GIFTS FOR
YOUR SEASONS

GIFTS FOR
YOUR SEASONS

*Inspirational Thoughts
for Life's Journey*

PAULINE OXLEY

To order additional copies of this book, contact:
Xlibris
UK TFN: 0800 0148620 (Toll Free inside the UK)
UK Local: (02) 0369 56328 (+44 20 3695 6328 from outside the UK)
www.Xlibrispublishing.co.uk
Orders@Xlibrispublishing.co.uk
821491

CONTENTS

ACKNOWLEDGEMENTS

The book has been written in memory of my late parents, Eudora and Alphonzo Oxley, whose simple lifestyle taught me to unwrap God's gift of contentment. It is also dedicated to my six siblings and brother posthumously. Over the years, their love, commitment, and sacrifice were gifts that have kept me along the way and brought me to this moment.

I dedicate this book to my daughter and son. They are amongst my most precious gifts that I have had the blessing of parenting.

The book is also dedicated to my two granddaughters and great-granddaughter.

I would like to thank all those who have read and edited the draft manuscript. Their helpful support has been invaluable and appreciated.

Names of friends are anonymous to protect their identity, and special thanks is given for their willingness to be mentioned in this book.

The Biblical texts being used throughout come from the New Kings James Version of the Holy Bible (NKJV).

1

INTRODUCTION

There are diversities of gifts, but the same Spirit
1 Corinthians 12:4

This book deals with the intangible gifts that God has given us and made available to everyone throughout the seasons of your life. They are gifts so they are not earned, but we can enjoy the benefits and results when we tap into God's gift box.

There are many questions I often ask myself such as what is my gift? How will I know that I have it, and how will others be able to recognise it, or how can it be used for the benefit of others?

What a beautiful way to begin the day knowing that despite all these burning questions about what gifts you may have, you are loved by the Creator of the universe who has invested so many expressions of love to make you a happy and contented person for every season of your life!

One of the main motivating factors for writing *Gifts for Your Seasons* is essentially to share my early-morning reflections while allowing these thoughts to distil into my day as I meditate on the Bible verses that have been specially selected for these themes.

These gifts are Bible-based, connected with personal journals, so it is fitting that these gifts should be returned to God in recognition as a loan and not my own (Tozer). They have become the fabric of who I am, being mixed with emotions, whether 'physiological or spiritual' (Seagalove).

Gifts for Your Seasons is about valuing the contribution you can make through essentials that enrich the varying seasons of life and make a difference to you, your family and community. They are designed to fit in well with who you are and your personality.

The gifts are intentionally provided by the Holy Spirit and are applicable to the present-day time that we are living in. It is clear that not all gifts come ready wrapped in material things, and there are a variety of intangible gifts to suit every age, background, social standing and abilities.

Identifying them as a God-given gift provides the strength to navigate the way that leads to fulfilment and satisfaction. Having these gifts gives direction instead of wandering aimlessly with doubts and fears when roadblocks are encountered along the way, like a sudden health challenge or the loss of a job.

Jesus has promised many blessings that are gift wrapped for every day and these gifts bring delightful experiences. My part is to accept these gifts unequivocally. The gifts come packaged with the promise of His Presence..

Jesus has promised many blessings that are gift-wrapped for every day, and these gifts bring delightful experiences. That depends not on affordability but on the gracious acceptance of His wealth and His pleasure to give these gifts. As the bountiful Giver, He is pleased to give the kingdom to us (Luke 12:32), and as a loving Father, He delights in giving gifts to His children.

In this book, I have shared inspirational thoughts and memories that have helped me to appreciate the gifts which are applicable to any season in life. It comes with a sense of thankfulness for what can be achieved through God's grace and power and the importance of living a life of contentment for what has been given.

As you delve into this book, you can either read in sequential order, or if you decide, you can dip into a section that piques your interest or mood on a particular day. They are available for any season you may be in right now.

There is no need to compare your gift with others. All the gifts that are mentioned in this book are possible to unwrap through the grace of God and not within your own power. It is a daily choice and challenge to discover each of the gifts according to God's promise.

By focusing on the Holy Spirit to help in finding the gift, whatever it may be, the gift/s will be given in direct relation to your struggles and limitations that are being experienced. It is only through prayer and asking God to reveal the best way of using the gifts that they begin to unfold.

God-given gifts, freely granted for His glory, are part of the daily decision and best used when shared and fine-tuned to bring out the ultimate purpose for those who have discovered the gift.

The examples given of how God has worked with Bible characters are inspiring. They include people like Paul, Ruth, Joseph, Abraham, and many others. They have been a source of personal encouragement. His intelligent design in creation, His faithfulness, and His loving character showcase His benevolent nature.

"Gifts for your seasons" invites you to reflect on Jesus' love, the greatest love of all, and is something to be treasured. I have found the Bible to be a precious gift because it provides instruction and guidance in times of uncertainty and throughout every season of my life.

The Bible provides invaluable lessons that unfold to provide instruction and guidance in all times of uncertainty and seasons.

The gift of health is a challenge to honour the body that has been given, and the gift of peace has a transforming stillness through the seasons of life. I cherish the gift of faith that helps me to see beyond what is happening and builds assurance and hope for the future.

Bible stories have been woven into each gift as a significant part in the experiences I have shared and how I can journey through life in the knowledge that although my challenges are not unique, they are personal to me.

It is my hope that as you reflect on the aspect of these gifts, the sense of contentment will empower you to accept God's benevolence in giving us good gifts. I have posed a question at the start of each section for you to contemplate on as a form of reflection and part of your own journaling project.

Diversity of Gifts

There is a subtle distinction between skills and the diversity of spiritual gifts. Skills are intended to show natural abilities and can be gained through training and usually inherited (Day). Talents are given by God, and can be developed and fine-tuned to perfection with practice, like the man who asked someone to tell him the way to Carnegie Hall and was told, 'practice, practice, practice.'

The litmus test of a spiritual gift is sometimes knowing that it is something that you enjoy doing or have a natural inclination towards. Spiritual gifts are specifically given by God as an added blessing, empowered through the Holy Spirit. They can sometimes be quite unexplainable and often through inspiration, vision, and wisdom (e.g. an effective spiritual leader, like the biblical leader Moses).

Whether or not it is recognised, everyone has been given a gift or a variety of gifts for the journey as we travel through life and its myriad of experiences. Due to our individual choices, the gifts can be accepted as part and parcel of the blessings that are ours every day of our lives. We need to understand the significance of the gifts that we are given.

By divine wisdom, God knows how to give individualised gifts to everyone who asks. They are given with a willingness to use and accept the gift or gifts with gratitude. There is no partiality as Jesus said that 'if you then, being evil, know how to give good gifts to your children, how much more will your Father who is in heaven give good things to those who ask him!' (Matthew 7:11).

The saying is true that we lose what we fail to use, so the gift/s must be utilised and not compared to the gifts of others. Once the gift/s is/are unwrapped, the process of using them becomes a daily adventure. The challenges of life require strength to use them. God delights in seeing our faces light up as we experience the surprise of knowing that He thought about our gifts a long time before we did!

Whatever inspires you to use your gift should be used as a tool to do something artistic and original with your new-found ability, which can be something that comes naturally, with little or no effort, or something that is cultivated but based almost always on inspiration and enjoyment.

Priorities of life undoubtedly reflect the importance we place on them. The human experience is one that is full of ups and downs, good days and not so good days. These are seasons that the book addresses as the gifts are unwrapped to help cope with the uncertainties of life and what it presents to us.

2

MY MOTHER'S BIBLE

*For prophecy never came by the will of man, but holy men
of God spoke as they were moved by the Holy Spirit.*
2 Peter 1:21

How has the Bible inspired and shaped your life? If someone you knew did not believe in the Bible, what would be your best experience in favour of its relevance today?

The Bible and the inspiration of the Holy Spirit is where it all starts in discovering spiritual gifts. My late mother first introduced me to the Bible as a child growing up to learn the familiar stories like David and Goliath, Samson, Joseph and his coat of many colours, the miracles that Jesus performed, the story of Jesus's birth, the creation, and of course, the gift of God's love on the cross and many more. From that time on, I experienced the Bible as a source of inspiration.

My mother's extensive knowledge of God's Word formed the principles on which she lived, and she never missed an opportunity to share and explain anything I did not understand. The Bible had been her constant companion, and it became equally precious to me. Throughout my life, she would encourage me to deepen my knowledge of the Word for guidance and inspiration along life's journey. It was her precious gift that she gave to me that we enjoyed reading every day together and she would often advise me to 'feed the soul' by daily study of the Bible.

She knew that the Bible, above all else, would be the single, most sustaining source of strength to face the future. Towards the end of her life, the regular visits to her one-bedroom accommodation at the care home in Letchworth, Hertfordshire, were always moments when she would share the Word of God, and we often prayed together. She looked forward to family visits, which brightened up her day. I recall on one occasion when I organised a prayer session at the home. This was the last time my mother and I exchanged any meaningful communication.

She was at peace at the end of her life. She was a phenomenal woman of prayer and knew the Bible well. She also knew how to start the day with faith and expectation. During her lifetime, I recall my mother's untiring desire to unwrap this precious gift of contentment through daily devotion and encouraging me to join her at her bedside for daily prayer times. I admired her faith as a scholar of the Word, and her example led me to search the Scriptures for myself.

The Bible became one of the most precious gifts that I have been motivated to read above all other genre, important as they are. I began to memorise verses, which provided me with a moral compass through which I could navigate God's will for my life when I needed it. It was written by men who were inspired by the Holy Spirit to write down what they saw, heard, and experienced.

My earliest memories of unwrapping this precious gift of my mother's Bible were due to daily Scripture reading at home, regularly attending a Baptist Church in Barbados, and being involved in children's activities. It was a time when the church provided children with fun things to do during the summer holiday and became the main social outlet for most families. I remember learning and reciting Scripture verses. This included competitions, resulting in prizes and certificates. This reinforced a positive feeling of achievement from an early age and created within me the desire to know the Bible more.

I have experienced that the Bible can bring hope and comfort despite trials, disappointments, and encouragement in times of joy and happiness. It meets all my needs for encouragement and communication with God, through which He speaks to me.

The Bible is an inspirational book because it gives a clear picture of the triumphs as well as the mistakes of ordinary people while meeting the needs for physical, emotional, and spiritual healing. It inspires me in many practical ways. I find it to be a Book that encourages and uplifts my spirit, with many promises that I can claim. It contains God's law, and at the same time, I see His love shining through its many truths like a thread.

The Bible accomplished many convictions in my life as a believer in getting to know the Author, what God is like and His character. It became a book that would satisfy my deep longing for love, support, and purpose. It provides a healing solace which uplifts and encourages me every time I study it.

I recall back in 2018 when I became concerned about my dreams. They may not have had any particular significance, simply a replay of what had been happening during the day. These dreams were persistent and consistent with the thought of fear or helplessness. These dreams would seem to indicate that I was almost ready for something but not quite ready, for example, getting dressed for an occasion but not being at the event or being due to sing or read a poem but not having the words.

I turned to the Bible for an answer to my dreams and to find out how God could show me the meaning of these dreams that I kept having. God can also use dreams as He did in the past. I found reassurance in reading Isaiah 41:10, which says, 'Fear not, for I am with you, be not dismayed, for I am your God. I will strengthen you, yes I will help you. I will uphold you with my righteous right hand.' That verse gave tremendous reassurance, and I realised that these dreams were showing me my need of someone to strengthen and uphold me.

Its truths are embedded in sound principles and have survived the years as the only book that lives for the present as well as the past and future. It looks back in time to the beginning and spans the history of centuries, leaping into the future and the end of time itself. It contains knowledge 'and is profitable for doctrine, for reproof, for correction, for instruction in righteousness' (2 Timothy 3:16).

The Bible has been proven to me to be an active book of discoveries for present-day living. It involves searching and finding, and in doing so, it becomes relevant to the reader. At one point, I found it easier to start at the beginning in Genesis and work my way through the book, but this has not consistently worked out that way. Reading it randomly is not the most recommended method for me, but when I am looking for quick answers, I tend to focus on a particular book and work through that for a while.

Whenever I am engaged in Bible study, I find God's purposes shining through. In the past, I tended to avoid some books of the Bible, like Revelation and Daniel, because of lack of understanding. I am beginning to study these two Books and finding them to be relevant to end time prophecy which give an accurate picture of predictions for the future. This brings hope and comfort that things will eventually be rectified from a world of conflict and confusion to a brighter tomorrow. The battle between good and evil is still prevailing and is stronger than ever, with issues like moral decline to be an ever-present dilemma. Developing a sense of order in how I approach the Word of God is helpful. It has become a reliable source of truth, authority, and trustworthiness.

My mother's gift of the Bible and encouraging me to get to know God by reading and studying it has been one of the most amazing gifts I have ever received. When she died peacefully on 20 July 2003, my mother's Bible was closely held by her bedside.

As believers, the Bible encourages us to 'be diligent to present yourself approved to God, a worker who does not need to be ashamed, rightly dividing the word of truth' (2 Timothy 2:15).

3

CONTENTMENT

Be anxious for nothing
Philippians 4 v 6

Whathat is your understanding of contentment?

The road to happiness has many avenues, and a life that is centred on contentment is a way that is travelled by those who find pleasure and gratification despite having little or much to be happy about. Regardless of one's situation in life, the ability to value life as more important than either money, status, or other material things can make a tremendous difference to the way we live.

I was raised in a Christian home. My recollection of my childhood was happy and stress-free. I lived in a place of sea and sun, and every day was a beautiful childhood experience to reflect on as a truly pleasurable time while growing up in those early years.

Most of the parental influence in the home was due to the devotion and commitment of my mother, who guided me through all aspects of my development, in the areas of physical, spiritual, educational, and social development.

I was 14 years old when my father died. His sudden death due to pancreatic cancer had a devastating effect on me and was the beginning of a season that was hard to come to terms with.

Church life was a major feature, and I was encouraged to follow principles that laid the foundation for the life to follow.

There were many challenges during my formative years; however, there was satisfaction despite having limited material things, finding the security and comfort within a loving family unit. There was a sense of humour that helped to diffuse many challenges that were faced. I experienced contentment and appreciation for what life had to offer me.

Living a life of contentment meant that even a lack of material things did not affect my enjoyment of life, as I learned even at that young age that life had more to do with values than mere things that I could not afford. Its unity and moral compass always made me feel safe and appreciated. I wondered then and now how you could have so little and yet find happiness and satisfaction in what you have.

Accepting the free gifts of peace, cheerfulness, and a sense of well-being, of which contentment is defined, can have an impact on our lives. By giving recognition to the blessings of the things we have rather than what we do not have can help to put things into perspective in living a contentment-centred life.

The English writer Samuel Johnson gives an interesting view of contentment. He said that it relates to our perspective on life. It begins in the mind and our emotional attachment to things. Contentment involves an attitude of a positive mindset. It begins and ends with the conviction that the only thing we can truly own is our response to life and what happiness really means.

Johnson explains the thought that the more we strive to change external things around us while neglecting the issue of self-change, the more we will find ourselves in a wasteful exercise. The very happiness we are seeking cannot be achieved unless it comes from within.

What is it that makes for true contentment? It may be reasonable to say that contentment leads to a peaceful way of thinking that promotes a sense of appreciation for what you have. It asks for no more than the ability to enjoy life without comparing yourself with others who may have more. Contentment is a stress reliever and removes feelings of inferiority or inequality, with the resolve to live within your means.

I believe that God's decisions about my future are infinitely more important than mine. The gift of contentment results in less pressure and the need to be consumed with gaining things that I cannot afford. With the big overview in front of Him, Jesus can guide me along the path if I am willing to be co-operative with His plan.

> There are always lessons I can learn from claiming the gift of contentment; one of which is an appreciation of what I have rather than what I want. Of course, this does not mean settling for less or giving up the ability to strive for better things, which is an admirable goal. The gift of contentment continues to offer me the ability to cope with times of abundance as well as times of restricted resources.

We hear the figures of the richest people in the world, and to ask them the secret of their successful lives would reveal hard work, maybe, or inheritance. The accumulation of wealth does not make a man great. In the eyes of God, greatness comes from being known as a God-fearing person and one who lives in the way God wants you to.

Life during the global pandemic of 2020–2021 due to COVID-19 has been a challenging time in terms of contentment. It has reinforced the precedence of needs above wants and the preservation of life as the primary essential need. I learned how to do without things I do not need, for example, shopping for clothes that are seldom worn anyway.

I once heard a story of a servant who was happy and contented with his life. The king was curious about his happiness and his constant singing yet having so little to sing about. The king decided, after seeking some advice, to give him ninety-nine gold coins, which made the servant overjoyed.

However, the servant, having ninety-nine gold coins, became consumed with wanting the hundredth coin. He worked hard, and not long afterwards, his whole personality changed. He stopped singing as he continued to strive for the missing coin. He soon lost the essence of that which brings true happiness. The one missing coin became more important than the gift of contentment with the ninety-nine.

God grants riches, so they are good, provided they do not defame the character and personality. Contentment brings the reality of the most essential things in life. The story of the missing gold coin being a case in point because God has promised to 'supply all your needs according to His riches in glory by Christ Jesus' (Philippians 4:19).

Many years ago, I worked for an engineering firm. Two of the employees, an engineer and an electrician, teamed up in placing weekly bets on the lottery. They both had high hopes of what they would do if they won it. Everything they ever wanted would be affordable.

One day, their fortune finally came when they had lucky numbers and won quite a substantial amount of money. They divided their windfall equally between them. The engineer immediately resigned from his job and decided to waste his portion by gambling and drinking until the money was gone.

The electrician decided to invest it in purchasing other properties and completely renovated them. Quite a contrast in the way they responded to their windfall. I could not help thinking about the man who wasted his money and allowed it to destroy him. The Bible tells us, 'For the love of money is a root of all kinds of evil, for which some have strayed from the faith in their greediness and pierced themselves through with many sorrows' (1 Timothy 6:10). True satisfaction and contentment to live within your means reduce feelings of greed as opposed to need.

Experiencing hardships in my formative years made a significant inroad to the way I value life more than material possessions. This became a massive source of learning to appreciate scarcity and plenty, treating both extremes with the same level of acceptance. I learned that life had more to do with how we relate to each other and how much fun I had growing up, and those happy memories sustained the feeling of what really matters in life.

I was happy because the gift of contentment provided satisfaction to make me feel safe. I appreciated the importance that God provides for our needs and tells us not to spend time worrying. It helped me to resist the temptation to complain, which is usually described as the dark room where Satan develops his negatives.

One of my favourite Bible characters is the apostle Paul. His journey of unwrapping the gift of contentment was expressed in his understanding of the feeling of happiness with whatever came his way in life. It was not the abundance of things that made him feel secure;

he reckoned the essence of having either little or much should not define him or his values.

Paul's circumstances were placed within the context of God's provision and plan; therefore, he had no need to be unnecessarily ambitious about material gain or comparing himself with others. He met them both with confidence in his ability to avoid letting either of them overwhelm him. He said, 'I know how to be abased, and I know how to abound. Everywhere and in all things, I have learned both to be full and to be hungry, both to abound and to suffer need' (Philippians 4:12).

The materialistic world in which we live deprives us of the joy of happiness. The struggle for competing, keeping up with others, and wanting more and more is a consuming malady of our society that denies us serenity. It can drive us to a state of avarice where nothing satisfies.

Jesus once gave a parable of a rich man who became wealthy through the successful yielding of his crops. He ran out of room to store them and began a rebuilding programme of taking down barns and building new and greater ones so that he could continue to accumulate his wealth and store it up for himself. He then decided he would take it easy and enjoy his life. However, in that very night, God's response was that his soul would be required of him that night (Luke 12:20).

One night a rich young ruler once came to Jesus and posed the question about getting eternal life (Matthew 19:16). Jesus responded by telling the man that to receive eternal life, obedience to the commandments is necessary, to which he asked, 'Which ones?' Jesus then outlined the Ten Commandments to him, and the young ruler claimed that he had been keeping them since he was young and wanted to know if there was anything else that he lacked.

The question 'What can I do to inherit eternal life?' suggests that he thought it was possible to earn salvation. Therefore, Jesus corrected the young man by reminding him that putting Jesus first is the number one requirement above all other things, like the wealth he had been clinging on to.

Hence, Jesus's responded that it was harder for a camel to go through the eye of a needle than for a rich man to enter God's kingdom. The man walked away disappointed because he was rich and had a lot to lose because of his possessions (Matthew 19:22).

For this young searcher of eternal life, there was a desire to earn his way into heaven by the question 'What shall I do?' Having been raised to observe the law fully, he felt that there was something missing, just one more thing he must do, so he asked Jesus for the answer.

Jesus immediately gave him the choice to follow Him, by prioritising the things that would keep him from becoming a sincere follower. He would have to let go of whatever was standing in the way of true worship as it required giving up on the things that were cherished dearly that would hinder and be a distraction.

The rich young man professed his thorough knowledge and observance of the Ten Commandments, but top of the list was the commandment to have no other gods. His sorrowful reaction would indicate that he was not prepared to give that up, but with all his material goods, it did not satisfy his longing for a better life, because 'as white is to black, so is contentment to complaints and anxiety' (MacArthur).

The reflection for me in this story is the fact that God wants me to put Him first in my life and let go of anything that would hinder my access to Him and my relationship with Him. In doing so, I can worship Him alone and be contented with whatever life has to offer me.

He can and will supply all your needs for a satisfying life, whatever the season, be it social, emotional, physical, or spiritual, and satisfy the longing for a meaningful relationship with Him. This then negates that question, what more do I lack? This is the greatest need of all that is met by the gift of contentment.

4

SELF-WORTH

Do not fear therefore, you are of more value than sparrows
Matthew 10:31

W hat do you see about yourself that promotes your value and sense of self-worth?

Self-worth is defined by Merian-Webster's dictionary as a sense of your value as a human being. It is based on how you feel about yourself as an individual as opposed to anyone else. Failure to recognise ourselves the way Christ values us may derive from many experiences in the past that have affected our low esteem or feeling that we are not good enough. We tend to see ourselves through other people's lens, which impacts our confidence and self-esteem. Yet our worth and acceptance is in Jesus Christ, which results in a healthy commitment (Brand and Yancey).

More than twenty years ago, before my mother's death, she gave me the gift of a British £5 coin which had just been recently issued in 1990. Over the years, I have kept the coin safely tucked away, until recently, when I began to think about that coin and how much it would be worth thirty-one years later.

The gift of this coin got me thinking about self-worth in terms of how much I am worth to God. Does He value me like a coin that increases in value as time goes on? Or is His estimation of me unchanging, timeless, and precious, regardless of the season I am in? I therefore do not increase in value like an old coin; I am highly valued from beginning to end. A virtuous woman is described in the Bible as being worth more than rubies.

A nineteenth-century American poet named Myra Brooks Welch, who died in 1959, wrote a well-known poem called '*The Touch of the Master's Hand*' or '*The Old Violin*'. I can never forget the first time this poem was read. It is a beautiful illustration of self-worth.

The poem recounts an old man who took a violin to an auction to be sold. The violin looked like it had seen better days and was described as 'battered and scarred'. Its price was going for no more than $3.00. as the auctioneer cried out for a price.

There was an old man sitting at the back of the room who got up and started to take the old violin. As he dusted it off and adjusted the strings, he played a beautiful tune that was 'pure and sweet', which amazed the auctioneer and the crowds. The value of the violin rose from $3.00 to $3,000. The secret of the instrument was the touch of its owner and master, who knew the true value of the violin. If I am ever unsure of my worth, the gentle touch of my Father's hand will reassure me.

We know that the body is an intricate and perfect creation, and this places a high value on our worth. Like the old violin, even when we are broken by emotional or physical pain, the created model of human life is still of high value.

Love motivated Jesus to go to Calvary to reinstate my relationship with Him towards growth and self-worth and the need for contentment of His plan in my life. There are countless times when I feel totally overwhelmed by God's love and acceptance of me, and I try to see myself as a valuable human being with infinite worth and ability. He values my worth because He knows how much effort was put into my makeup, so I just need to accept the fact that He loves me just the way I am, accepted and free to love myself with an accurate level of self-worth.

The Holy Scriptures give many answers to justify our worth to God:

- We are made in His image. We are the only ones in all creation that is described in this way. Animals are ruled by instincts, but we are capable of thinking and reasoning. Isaiah 1:18 says, 'Come now let us reason together says the Lord, though your sins are like scarlet they shall be white as snow, though they are red like crimson, they shall be as wool.'

- Jesus died and gave His life for us (John 3:16).
- He made us a little lower than the angels and crowned us with honour and glory (Hebrews 2:7).
- The psalmist asked the question, 'What is man that You are mindful of him?' (Psalm 8:4).
- He has invited us to the banqueting table, and His banner over us is love (Song of Solomon 2:4).
- He told us not to worry about tomorrow because He will care for us.

Notwithstanding imperfections and limitations, I am still extremely valuable to God. In His estimation, no one is a mistake. Every human being has a high value to God because He has placed a huge investment in His creation, so 'I will praise You for I am fearfully and wonderfully made' (Psalm 139:14).

In God's economy, we are valuable, and the cross is proof of that. Every human being has a worth that is of high value to God because He made us and He is familiar with who we are. The price that He paid through His blood on Calvary is the evidence of how much we are worth to Him. Therefore, we can declare self-worth as a special gift.

Jesus said that we are worth dying for, and even in our sinful state, He still believes in our potential to become changed and to reflect His character in all His purity and splendour.

As I travel through the various stages and seasons of life, I need to be cognisant of the incredible importance to God and to others. This will make a tremendous impact on my self-worth. Consequently, my attitudes and behaviour will reflect that value of being worthy of love and approval.

I reflect the example of what He wants me to be, and although I accept my unworthiness of His high unconditional regard for me, He is still willing to invest in my future and heal the scars, repair the brokenness, cover the blemishes, fill the emptiness, and reshape the damaged self-image.

One such person was a woman whom Jesus met as He travelled on foot from Judea to Galilee via Samaria, north of Jerusalem. He made a diversion because there was a Samaritan woman who needed to be given the opportunity to reinstate her value as a person despite her lifestyle (John 4).

The story began when Jesus met a Samaritan woman at the well called Jacob's Well. This was in the neighbourhood of Sychar, near a plot of land which Jacob had bequeathed to his son Joseph for supplying water to his descendants and cattle. His conversation with the Samaritan woman revolutionised her life that day.

He seemed to know all there was to know about her without her personal disclosure, but there was no condemnation in His conversation with her. He commented and revealed to her that He knew all about her and the fact that she had been married five times and was now cohabiting with a man who was not her husband, a custom which was scorned upon in the culture of her day.

'Give me a drink,' Jesus asked her, which left her surprised as there was a cultural barrier that prevented Jews from associating themselves with Samaritans. Jesus, at this time, was in a state of exhaustion from the heat, being an extremely hot noon day. He needed to quench His physical thirst. At this point, Jesus allowed her to draw water for Him.

It would have been her custom to go to the well before the other women came along. As Jews did not associate with Samaritans (John 4:9), she must have felt the pain of being an outcast, filled with shame and scorn from the neighbouring women. She was weighed down not only by her bucket of water but also by the stigma of a personal crisis that left her feeling low on self-worth.

With a social background of failed relationships, Jesus met her and restored her dignity and self-worth. I can only imagine that she felt stigmatised by her own inability to maintain a healthy view of herself. In this season of her life, the timing was right for change and the timing was right to receive the gift of self-worth. She accepted the challenge when Jesus announced, 'Whoever drinks of the water that I shall give him will never thirst.' She then implored Him, 'Sir, give me this water that I may not thirst, nor come here to draw' (John 4:15).

The kind of water that Jesus was offering her was a fulfilled life that would give her an innate sense of her value. Her opinion of herself had been based on how others viewed her. She needed a conviction of self-respect and as someone whose life could be viewed in the light of God's opinion of her. This would counteract the value that society had placed on her as a Samaritan woman. On her own, she could never measure up, but by accepting the Living Water, she was given a new value of her importance. She would never thirst again, and this was what she needed. It would lead to eternal life, which she was willing and ready to accept as the gift of renewed self-worth.

This was a new and exciting experience that made her leave the water-pots of her past life. She ran into the city to invite others to come and meet Jesus. Her hunger for a change was met with love and acceptance. She now felt confident to go and share the good news to those she once shunned. Maybe for the first time, she met a man who did not condemn her but introduced her to a new value of herself.

Upon reflecting on this issue of self-worth, I remember one day when I picked up a free *Metro* newspaper on my way home from work. My attention was immediately drawn to an article called 'Cracking Result as Chipped Vase Urns Its Owner £87K'. It was a report of a floral vase that was broken, and the owner felt embarrassed to have it on show in the house.

The antique was hidden away in the garage for ten years, after which time she decided to take it to a charity event as she considered it to be useless with the crack in it. She felt that the broken vase had no worth or value.

While she was on her way to give away her broken urn, she stopped in at an auctioneer's valuation day, and as fortune would have it, the auctioneer examined the vase and suggested an online sale by Eastbourne Auctions. A Chinese buyer saw the twelve-inch vase and immediately recognised it to be a vase that was designed for a Chinese emperor and its apparent worth in the region of £500M. Due to the crack, the vase was sold to the owner for £87K. The value of the vase was reduced by the crack so that its value, once cracked, was of less worth.

The gift of self-worth reinforces the fact that even though there are cracks and brokenness, we are not beyond repair. Those imperfections do not determine our worth, and our value is never diminished simply because we have experienced brokenness and are bruised by the seasons of life and its reasons that may try to disfigure self-image. We may be bruised but still within the care of One who is able to repair the damage and make us new again.

There is a tendency to base self-worth on what we acquire and accumulate as material wealth. One of the wealthiest women in the world is the celebrity Oprah Winfrey. In her book *What I Know for Sure*, she came to realise that self-worth was not dependent on having the best car. She shared the conviction that there was a time when having the best things in life made her feel like the best. She later discovered that having the best was not a substitute for having the best life.

The story is told of an American tourist who purchased an inexpensive amber necklace in a jeweller shop while in Paris. He was shocked when he had to pay quite a high duty on it to clear Customs in New York. This aroused his curiosity, so he had it appraised. After looking at the object under a magnifying glass, the jeweller said, 'I'll give you $25,000 for it.' Greatly surprised, the man decided to have another expert examine it. When he did, he was offered $10,000 more!

'What do you see that was so valuable about this old necklace?' asked the astonished man. Looking through this glass before his eyes was an inscription from Napoleon Bonaparte to Josephine. The value of the necklace came from its identification with a famous person unknown.

God has already placed the gift of self-worth that gives us the ability to see ourselves as He sees us. It does not depend on external factors but on knowing who you are and whose you are. I know the expensive value of this gift as it comes with the highest price of His life. No one can eradicate the stamp of worth that has been placed on me.

Being treated with respect and dignity helps to promote self-worth. Relying on others' opinion can be soul destroying as efforts to live up to others' expectations of you, apart from our own value system, can diminish the worth that God has placed in us. The impact of negative comments and unkind words can damage self-worth and can affect behaviours that lead to low self-worth and low self-esteem. Believing in yourself can build confidence and help to maintain a healthy opinion of yourself, regardless of what others say to you and about you.

Through Christ, we are valuable and of great worth, with an accurate estimation of ourselves, regardless of whatever season we are in. This gives the assurance that despite the human sinful nature, He has a high value on His masterpiece (us). This is something that is undeserving, but nonetheless, God's pleasure is perfected as He restores the broken life. He promises to deal with the whole person, spirit, soul, and body, and He wants to preserve us until He comes again.

5

COURAGE

Fear is an emotion; courage is a decision
Winston Churchill

How does God speak to you through the gift of courage, and how has this gift enabled you to conquer fear?

The bravery of many has been forever etched in the halls of fame, as those who will stand up and be counted and their attitude and fortitude throughout history are worthy of honour. Such is the memory of Winston Churchill, a leader and prime minister whose inspired and courageous words led to the victory during the Second World War.

There are some important things that I have learned about courage. It begins with a decision, and once the decision is made, the emotion gives way to the courage that dispels the fear associated with doing the thing that you most feared.

The book *Feel the Fear and Do It Anyway* by Susan Jeffers was a book that helped me to conquer the belief that I could overcome uncertainties of what I can become and accept the gift of courage. Jeffers talked about the no-lose decision-making process. This involves meeting each season in life in a positive way and trusting in God-given capabilities.

Jeffers also advised that 'the knowledge that you can handle anything that comes your way is the key to allowing yourself to take healthy, life-affirming risks'.

The story of Rosa Parks, the African American lady, has always been a source of inspiration to me and relates to the gift of courage. She was someone who was not afraid to take risks and be courageous. She stepped out with an audacity that defied those around her and demonstrated the willpower to be a woman of exemplary raw courage. She lived in a time of racial hatred and discrimination in a town in the United States called Montgomery and died in 2005.

From the humble beginning as a seamstress who loved her job, Rosa used the bus to travel to and from work. Her courage became historic for black people who might be afraid to stand up for what they believe in. As a visionary, she believed in the equality of all people, and her sense of fairness and justice made her refuse to sit at the back of the bus because of discrimination. Her courage was demonstrated in the face of segregation, which began a boycott, led to the Civil Rights Act in 1964, and consequently brought freedom against the injustice of discrimination.

Winston Churchill's quotation is a true one, which says that fear is only an emotion, which only goes away when the decision is made to be courageous. In fact, it is that decision that helps you to act on your emotions and overcome the fear.

The determination to be one of many who will acknowledge courage to be a gift is inspirational. Courageous people do not usually count the cost of their outstanding ability to forge ahead and become iconic examples for us to follow. We can see it in the courage of a young Olympic swimmer who defies age and meets the challenge to become a gold medallist or the experience of a thirteen-year-old who achieved the 2021 skateboarding bronze in the Tokyo Olympics. They know the secret of being a single voice with a single goal which does not deter them from following their dream.

One of the many biblical stories of courage is recorded in Numbers 13. A couple of courageous men named Joshua and Caleb were assigned by God through Moses, the leader of the Israelites, to act as spies before the Israelites could enter the promised land of Canaan. The Israelites had been on a journey after their massive and miraculous exodus from Egypt. The time had now come for them to enter the land that God had promised them.

The instruction was to choose a leader from each of the tribes from the wilderness of Paran. Moses was given the names of these men who would travel up the mountains in the south and have a look and see whether the inhabitants were strong or weak and how many there were.

The spies were recruited to report back on whether the land was fit for habitation and whether it was a wealthy, luscious place to live in. Moses commanded the spies to be courageous and to report back with samples of the fruit and what type of people were living there. It was the season of the first fruits (Numbers 13:18–20).

The expedition to spy out the land and the glowing and exciting reports revealed that it had everything. They were impressed by the strength of the people and the fortified cities; however, some of the men had a different perception on what they saw. They described the people as giants who made them look like grasshoppers in comparison to them!

The courageous Joshua and Caleb brought back an entirely different report; they saw opportunity instead of failure and strength instead of weakness. They saw a land that was 'an exceedingly good land', not people to be feared (Numbers 14:7–9).

The ability to overcome fear was also experienced by the apostle Peter as he accepted God's gift of courage when he launched into the deep water with Jesus. He was motivated to step out of the security of his boat and into the unknown. This must have been an incredible experience as he held on to Jesus, who beckoned to him to walk on the water with Him. Jesus questioned Peter's lack of faith when he looked at the waves and not on Jesus (Matthew 14:25–31).

Sometimes fear can take such a hold that it prevents memorable moments of courage from happening. Fear knocks for those on whose past it breeds, with the chilling voice of failure that causes us to lack courage and makes us see problems as bigger than they really are.

If we are daring like Joshua and fearless like Caleb, we too can accept the promised gift of courage. He who dares can affirm that he is not afraid of mistakes or failure. This is a challenge when we want to make a new start, to experience something new, but it potentially causes us to feel afraid.

The gift of courage is one that I can unwrap any time I sense the tendency to be fearful so that I can experience something quite miraculous that I would have missed had I given in to my fears. It enables you to stand out and stand alone with God and, in times of aloneness, to be able to conquer the giant of fear in a realistic way and turn it around to victory.

As I reflect on the effect that fear can bring, I recognise the need for God's strength to be positive and make a difference to whatever season you are going through. It may be the courage to give up on a habit that is impeding your ability to step out. I remember many times when Jesus spoke the words 'Fear not'. His words to Abraham was, 'Do not be afraid, Abram; I am your shield, your exceedingly great reward' (Genesis 15:1). To Isaac, Jacob's son, we read, 'I am the God of your father, Abraham, do not fear for I am with you. I will bless you and multiply your descendants for my servant Abraham's sake' (Genesis 26:24).

My decision today is to take all my concerns about courage to the Lord. To open them before Him and ask for His guidance in overcoming them. To see the fears not as giants but grasshoppers! God has the power to turn fears into an opportunity to do something great for Him.

In simple faith, He will do that. He can surmount the problems that seem difficult and turn doubts into His glorious possibilities. In stepping out, we contend with the enemy of fear and join forces with the One who has all-overcoming power to release courage into our lives.

> God has not given us a spirit of fear, but of power and of love, and of a sound mind. (2 Timothy 1:7)

6

CREATION

God dwells in His creation and is everywhere
indivisibly present in all His works.
A. W. Tozer

How does the gift of creation influence your relationship
with God?

The gift of creation, as recorded in the first book of the Bible,
Genesis, was God's most beautiful intention. He is visible in all His
creation, and its perfection is an undeniable gift, even in an imperfect
world with the spoils of man and climate change. The world has been
given to us to live in and explore as stewards of the vast universe that
He has made. It speaks of His power to create, restore, and recreate.
It is still a beautiful world, filled with wonder and amazement! It was
a gift of unimaginable original power that lit up the world in just six
days, and then God rested on the seventh day!

God made a world out of darkness and nothingness and populated
the sky with stars too numerous to mention. He commanded light
where there was darkness and created something out of nothing. His
was the voice of the true light that had come into our world. The Word
was spoken, and He was the life and light of men. He made daytime
and night-time, heaven and earth, seas and dry land. There were

animals of every kind and delicious fruit on every tree in the Garden of Eden, with numerous varieties of plants and herbs.

There were rippling rivers, mountains, hills, valleys, and miraculous splendour at the beginning of time when creation was birthed for the first time. In the spinning wheel of a vast cosmos, Earth was formed, with magnificent waterfalls and forests. It is truly a magnificent display of intelligent design.

I imagine the first night-time to give a cool, gentle breeze that began to caress the trees, and subtle shades of darkness fell below. All the created birds folded their wings as sounds of nightly creatures were heard. I imagine how the galaxy of stars then illumined the sky as the moon gave a splendid sight to see. The creation was beyond expression, and the Creator made a wonderful exhibition of the gift of creation. The world was full of the wonder of nature!

Amidst all the splendour at the masterful hand of the Creator, the best creation was man, whom He formed from the dust with His own hands, and He breathed into Adam's nostrils the breath of life. The divine Trinity became involved in the story of creation. There were seasons, all four, that were designed to follow each other in perfect order, the warmth of summer, the freshness of springtime, autumn glory and cold, wintry days.

The Garden of Eden was gifted to Adam and Eve and now to us one day. They had the freedom to enjoy all there was to enjoy in this awesome home. The creation of man was the crowning glory of it all!

A. W. Tozer, author of *The Pursuit of God*, remarked on the drastic change that took place between God and the relationship which had changed from a perfect union with His first created people. The change came when our fore parents made the grievous mistake about who they should obey. Tozer added that they had now adopted an 'altered attitude' towards God and so began the change from innocence to guilt.

From that moment on, sin began its rippling effect down the ages. What was once a beautiful garden of freedom now became a hiding place from their Maker (Genesis 3). Adam and Eve had enjoyed open fellowship with God. They heard His footsteps in the garden. They became afraid and ran away and hid themselves. I cannot begin to imagine what that must have been like, but by faith, He continues to walk and talk with me as I travel and unpack this gift.

Adam and Eve had been given everything they could ever wish for. They even had the honour of walking with God in the cool of the day. In such an ideal setting, life was perfect, but in a weak moment of temptation, it all changed. And by disobedience, the perfect union that they had with their Maker was gone. It was evident from then that sin separated us from God.

In the Garden of Eden, they were given perfect freedom to enjoy all the beauty of their new world. By eating the forbidden fruit, death would be the consequence. Through Satan's beguiling deception, Eve initially made the choice to go against what God had commanded, and together, she and her husband, Adam, collaborated in the act of disobedience. At that point, their curiosity was aroused with a desire to know the difference between good and evil (Genesis 3:5). Maybe at that point of temptation, they could have solicited God's help in overcoming the desire to disobey Him.

When I reflect on the unsearchable mystery of God in His creation, it takes me back to the year 2014 when I experienced His amazing creation during an adventure on a deep-water submarine, called the Atlantis Submarine, in Barbados. It happened during a holiday to celebrate my graduation with two of my siblings. The submarine went 150 ft below sea level so that we could see many of the sea creatures living there that are part of God's creation.

As I stepped on board the huge submarine to begin my two-hour underwater journey of the coral reefs, I was greeted by confident tour operators who provided a live commentary with the promise of a well-conducted experience that would be safe. I would now explore some of God's exciting sea life, viewing hundreds of amazing sea creatures of the deep waters in the comfort of an underwater submarine!

During that incredible trip, I was able to see underwater marine life as I had never seen it before and was amazed by God's creatures who have a life that is so far removed from our day-to-day life. There was life and activity happening way beneath the earth's surface. For most of the journey, I was awestruck at what life is like so deep underwater. Such is the magnificence of God's creation when He pronounced that there should be living sea creatures.

It was a thrilling experience to observe the corals that were illuminated, and at one point, the lights on the submarine were switched off so that all the passengers could see night life even more clearly.

> The beauty of the earth gives ample opportunities for exploring the beautiful world around us and enjoy His magnificent gift of beauty. God's faithfulness and promise of four seasons never fail. Sunshine and rain are both part of His making. He oversees and controls everything everywhere by His omnipotent and omniscient power. The gift of creation is worthy of praise and thanksgiving. These seasons are gift-wrapped to give pleasure, enjoyment and brighten up our lives.

Following Jesus Christ is like taking a submarine voyage to a deeper level with Him, where things that cannot normally be seen on the surface or behind the scenes become visible as His light shines into our hearts.

The Christian's hope is that one day a new morning will break forth and Jesus will return and prepare the way for eternal restoration to begin. His promise is to rekindle His fellowship with His people. The new heaven and earth will once again be a perfectly unspoiled world as it was at the beginning, and the gift of creation will be a lifelong reunion with the Creator and all those who accept the gift of His Son, Jesus Christ. All things will be made new again, and there will be no need to hide from the one who made us!

> Have you not known? Have you not heard? The everlasting God, the Lord, the Creator of the ends of the earth, neither faints nor is weary. His understanding is unsearchable. (Isaiah 40:28)

The gift of creation has made a significant influence on my relationship with God because I see Him as a creative Master of the universe who has the power to create and recreate everything. Nothing is beyond His power, and because He is the great Controller, His ways are beyond my human comprehension. I remain contented with His plan—a plan that promises us the best that heaven can afford—because His power is limitless and untiring.

7

FAITH

Blessed is the man who trusts in the Lord, and whose hope is
in the Lord. For he shall be like a tree planted by the waters,
which spreads out its roots by the river, and will not fear when
heat comes, but its leaf will be green, and will not be anxious
in the year of drought, nor will cease from yielding fruit.
Jeremiah 17:7–8

W hen has the gift of faith been very evident in your life?

The passage in Jeremiah 17 was given to me by my mother and
placed in my Bible for many years. It speaks about the result of putting
trust and hope in the Lord. It describes the one who trusts in the Lord
to be like a tree that is planted by the water and spreads out its roots
by the river.

Faith brings assurance and security. The analogy of a tree that is
planted where its roots go down deep as it spreads out and grows to
give shade to others is my best example of faith. The tree also provides
an illustration of someone who hopes in the Lord with a guarantee of
not being afraid of either heat or drought but, like the tree, continues
to be fruitful. It can withstand fierce winds except in a hurricane, of
course, that can threaten its survival if it is not securely rooted.

There is growth in the person who receives sustenance from the Water of Life. The heat and drought bring equal contentment because of the source of its strength. Faith helps the life to withstand the elements of seasons and storms. They may shake and try to uproot but cannot break the one who allows his life to be luscious through drinking the Water of Life.

The Biblical story recorded in Matthew 8 tells of a centurion who came to Jesus to ask for healing of his servant who was laying at home paralyzed and tormented. Jesus honoured his request and said that He would visit and heal the sick man.

The centurion, however, pointed out to Jesus that as a man of authority he only needed to speak the word to his soldiers, and they would obey. He did not feel worthy of Jesus' visit, and felt that in a similar way, Jesus needed only to speak the word and his servant would be healed. (Matthew 8:5-13)

Jesus was impressed by the centurion's level of faith which He said He had not found in Israel. Then Jesus pronounced healing as he spoke to the centurion to go on his way and his servant was healed instantaneously.

Faith was the gift that helped the centurion to believe that anything is possible when approaching a God who is omnipotent and omniscient. The centurion accepted the gift of faith by believing. It became a vehicle of hope that carried him through to the instantaneous healing of his servant. Hope therefore sees the invisible; it also feels the intangible and achieves the impossible (Helen Keller).

Through faith, the centurion had no doubts whatsoever and recognised that distance made no difference to Jesus. He just had to say the word and it would be done, just like his own experience as a ruler, but he had no power to heal anyone.

Faith paved the way for changes to take place so that you can say yes to challenges that come your way. One day a neighbourr and his wife, with whom I have had a friendly relationship over the years, spoke to me about my tree that happened to overlook their garden. They were concerned because the tree had now taken root to the extent that it was lifting the slabs under their patio. I agreed to do something about it, and he hastily offered to uproot the tree to resolve the problem. For many years, I had watched the tree grow as it put down roots. I was not aware of the extent of its depth until its effects were seen by my neighbour.

Regretfully, my tree had to be cut down, but the stump now remains. It is a reminder to me that faith can grow and give the grounding that others can witness but cannot totally destroy. The leaves may fall in autumn and may wither in winter or during storms, but the roots still remain solid if planted on good ground, securely connected to the vine, and ready to be rejuvenated when the spring and summer return.

I also compare faith to be like a father teaching his son or daughter to mend a bike or fix a problem with the car. The child depends on the expertise of the parent for advice on the best way to mend the bike. You just watch him work and do what he tells you, knowing that he is more skilled. It is from this standpoint that faith brings trust in a God that is all-knowing. In my moment of reflection, I realise that I must get to the place where I acknowledge that God is far more skilled at working out my problems than I am.

Having faith shows that you are available and willing to accept His gift of trusting Him. Faith works especially well when there are big decisions to make. It is at times like these that we need to pray and ask God for guidance. Faith in God then reassures us of His mighty hand in directing a good outcome, irrespective of whatever season you are in.

Exercising faith can be a difficult thing when there is a lack of confidence in God's ability to bring about change. However, He leads us along a path where everything works together for the highest good through an understanding of His power. In this regard, I submit my problems as they come to me each day and know that He has provided for me a new way. As He works things out, His creative hand of tapestry weaves every situation into a good result according to His timing.

Trusting in His ultimate purposes and divine will means handing over the problem to God and watching Him work it out. There must be a willingness to let Him take over step by step through the process of learning to trust Him all the way through every season.

Faith initiates miracles that might not otherwise happen in the ordinary course of life. When faith is in action, it can make our feet like those of the deer, one of the most endearing animals. Its swiftness and ability to jump into the air is driven by the power of its hind legs. They can turn sharply because the front legs are created to do so, and they enjoy the ability to run fast. It is what they do naturally!

Through faith, we can overcome obstacles. We can take an example from the deer, whose feet allow it to jump over whatever is in its way. It is important to remember that the gifted ability is granted to us to do amazing things through faith in His power. We can long for this gift, just like the deer pants for water.

Faith brings assurance for tomorrow and gives me hope which is much needed today. Amidst a world of dubious things, the only answer is faith that counteracts the doubts and, in its place, gives assurance and peace for a brighter future. One writer puts it like this: 'Worrying doesn't take away tomorrow's troubles; it takes away today's peace' (unknown).

Jesus compared faith to a mustard seed, which can grow from a tiny seedling that germinates and begins to bud. As the plant grows into 'full yellow bloom', it relies on moisture to help it to blossom. The longer it thrives, the greater the yield. Once it is planted, the mustard seed does not remain the same, provided it is watered and tended in an environment that generates growth.

My faith has a way of bringing the impossible into the realm of possibility, and suddenly, it is realised that the struggle of putting faith in something that seems incredible becomes a reality.

One such experience happened during lunch one perfectly sunny day. The day began with bright skies, pink and beautiful. After a night of mist and wetness, it was good to see the sunshine beaming through the window, making everything look fresh and new.

While enjoying the warm weather that afternoon, my phone rang, and to my surprise, it was a call from the presenter of a local radio station inviting me to share my book with his listeners. My faith suddenly came into reality as one of my goals to be on radio was about to happen. I accepted the invitation without hesitation.

After that initial experience on the radio, it resulted in further phone calls from the same presenter. God had chosen this time, through the channels of faith, for me to do some book reviews once a month as a volunteer on his radio programme. This exciting experience made me believe that faith and action go together. Our skills and abilities can be utilised at the right place, at the right time. I considered it to be an answer to prayer.

During this time, I was given several books each month to go away and read and then share a critical review of them with the listeners. Reviewing and making recommendations of other writers' work on the radio was nerve-racking initially, but the project was enjoyable, and I began to look forward to each session and felt confident with my recommendations. On these occasions, I had been able to witness for Christ. I was asked on one occasion after the show to pray for the listeners.

Dr Richard de Lisser wrote an interesting book called *The Credit Crunch Christian*. In the book, he described faith as 'a hard commodity in our faithless age' but states that Christians are expected to have faith in good as well as bad times. Faith therefore can be exercised in season and out of season and does not depend on things going well all the time, nor does it just work when times are taking a downturn.

God's faithfulness does not change depending on how we feel; neither does faith change depending on what we are experiencing. The psalmist admonishes us to 'commit your way to the Lord, trust also in Him. And He shall bring it to pass' (Psalm 37:5).

Faith shows confidence in God's ability to work on our behalf. Trusting in God can be applied to all situations where confidence in His ability and contentment in what He can do will enable a favourable outcome. Everything then works together perfectly for good as part of His plan.

My reflection has been to arrive at the place where God is acknowledged as far more skilled at working out problems than we are. With our very finite vision of the future, His ultimate purposes and divine will is only seen through the eyes of faith. It would seem prudent then to submit and watch Him work it out. As the 'Alpha and the Omega, the Beginning and the End, the First and the Last' (Revelation 22:13), there must be willingness to let Him lead step by step through the seasons of learning to trust Him all the way through.

I am thankful for the opportunity to accept faith as a valuable gift as part of my survival kit. He is worthy and faithful and will never fail because faith is based on His attributes of mercy and goodness.

8

FORGIVENESS

Bearing with one another and forgiving one another
if anyone has a complaint against another, even
as Christ forgave you, so you also must do.
Colossians 3:13

How has this gift helped you? What lessons can you share with others about forgiveness?

Alexander Pope once said that whilst it is human nature to make mistakes, we resemble the divine nature of God when we choose to forgive someone. This is quite true because forgiveness is a gift that heals brokenness. Whenever I am faced with the need to forgive someone, I usually assume that it is a way of letting the person off the hook. To forgive them gives the opportunity to act more in line with the divine nature that is inherent in all.

Alexander Pope's inspiring thought explains how fallible humans are and how it takes a divine nature to forgive, because at those times of forgiveness, we resemble the Almighty since 'we are most like God when we forgive' (Jonathan Lockwood Huie). It is also true that we are more critical of others than we are of ourselves, so our judgement of ourselves is based on good intentions and others by their behaviour (Covey).

Admittedly, there were some occasions in the past when my level of forgiveness was rated low. I found it hard to reconcile the reasons for others' behaviour towards me that I felt, in my opinion, was undeserved. There were even times of job rebuttals, emotional times when dealing with difficult people, situations that were caused by a lack of respect, or unfairness in the workplace that would justify my spirit of unforgiveness.

I came to the realisation that forgiveness is a means of letting go of the hook that tied me to the person's wrongdoing. For instance, someone once hurt me in a way that made it difficult to let go of the memory. It became a hook that kept me going back to the awful experience again and again.

I could not see that the memory of what happened to me was causing me fresh pain every time my mind returned to it. I wanted to make the person responsible for how I was feeling. In reality, I gave the individual the power to decide on how best I should spend my day, because thinking of the hurt only opened up fresh wounds.

The alternative solution was to pray for the 'cleansing fire that burns away old regrets and resentments' (Lockwood Huie) and to have a spirit of reconciliation by extending forgiveness to others or vice versa. This exchange can be a healing and therapeutic experience. It is a time to show love instead of trying to get even with the person or fostering feelings of resentment.

It is worth remembering that forgiveness is intended for our benefit, not the person who has wronged us. Have you ever heard of the man who spent many years looking for another man who had wronged him in order to kill him, only to be told one day that the offender had died some years ago. What a waste of time and energy that was.

It was once shared with me the experience of how someone was waiting for an opportunity to express how she felt towards a family member who constantly insulted her every time she saw her. She found it hard to fight back and held her peace, but anger has been lying dormant, waiting for the opportune moment to unleash her resentment towards her in return.

The reality is that the time will never come unless there is a willingness to resolve the offensive behaviour that had been directed towards her. She has not made the decision to confront and resolve the situation that could renew their relationship.

I empathised with her for the pain she was struggling with because of the personal and unresolved experience I was going through at the time. I felt the pain that had caused her tremendous feelings of anger, bitterness, and frustration over the years, which could be avoided if she cleared the air. Emotional pain can be difficult to deal with, and it is not easy to move from hurt to healing.

I tried to counsel her but knew in my heart that I was struggling in the same way, but it gave me the opportunity to pray about it and recognise my own failure of not being able to witness to her and offer her a way out of an unforgiving spirit. It was a humbling experience as I have since learned that it must happen in my own life first before I can offer support in this area to others.

I turned to my mother's Bible and found the example in the parable of the unforgiving servant in Matthew 18. When Peter asked Jesus how many times he should forgive his brother, if it should be up to seven times, Jesus responded by saying it should not be seven times but seventy times seven. Jesus then gave a powerful example of a king who was eager to cash in on those servants who owed him money.

He firstly confronted the man who owed him 10,000 talents, which, according to research, would equate to over $600m. He could not afford to repay the debt. His master then ordered for him to be sold along with his wife and children to gather enough money to repay the debt. The man fell before the master and pleaded with him to give him time to pay back all he owed. The master was compassionate towards him and decided to cancel the debt altogether and extended forgiveness towards him.

Being forgiven of his large debt, the man then went to a fellow servant who owed him much less, 100 denarii, which, in today's terms, would equal four months' wages. (Massey) This was considerably less than the amount he owed his master who cleared his debt in full. The unforgiving servant forgot the cancelled debt he had received and demanded that his fellow servant pay him what he owed him, refusing to accept his request for more time.

Ignoring the man's plea for compassion in giving him some time to pay it back, he was filled with an unforgiving spirit and had him put in prison until the debt was paid. When the master found out how the unforgiving servant had treated his fellow servant who owed him much less than he owed the master; he became angry and ordered the unforgiving servant to be placed in the hands of debt collectors until he paid all that was owed.

The lesson of forgiveness showed that the man who was owed a great deal of money was forgiven of his debt had a responsibility to extend graciousness and forgiveness to his fellow servant. Instead, he became demanding and forgot how much he had been forgiven of his own debt (Matthew 18:21–35).

Taking the choice to forgive and make restitution brings freedom that would not otherwise have been possible. I then considered the fact that in order to be at peace, I need to also respond by extending forgiveness to others and myself. The formula that Jesus gave of forgiving seventy times seven goes beyond the idea of counting the number of times I forgive someone. Therefore, forgiveness is a limitless attitude that requires a tolerant spirit. It needs to be an automatic response whenever forgiveness is required and needed in order to move forward.

Hearing the genuine words 'I'm sorry' can also go a long way for forgiveness to take place. Sometimes people are unaware of what they have done, and sometimes it is purposeful and intended to harm others. Forgiveness is therefore the remedy to be used for my benefit, not the other person who has wronged me. When we are in a position of being vulnerable, the conscious decision to avoid further exploitation is important.

During Jesus's earthly ministry, many situations were presented to Him which needed His forgiveness of those who had wrongly accused Him. Instead, He chose forgiveness, especially when confronted with those who wanted to challenge His authority and His Divinity and, even then, to crucify him.

He paid the ultimate penalty of death on the cross as He uttered these uncondemning words: 'Father forgive them for they do not know what they do' (Luke 23:34). Even at that point, Jesus had the opportunity for revenge, as He had the power to destroy those who were crucifying Him, but he silently and lovingly chose to take the path of forgiveness to be an example for me to follow.

Dr Lynn Ponton, author of the article 'What Is Forgiveness?' defines it as a way of letting go and refusing to seek revenge. Children especially find it easy to forgive. They find it easy to let go and are not inclined to hold grudges.

Dr Ponton further said that forgiveness is a personal gift that allows us to get on with our lives, without trying to find ways to get even or score points. The saying is true that time is a great healer. The anger may lessen as time goes on, and the emotions at the time begin to wane, but the wound can take many years to heal.

There is the challenge of forgiveness that calls for open and honest feelings about the situation and talking to the person. This gives them the opportunity to say 'I'm sorry, please forgive me' and move on. These are not easy steps and require a level of maturity to take the lead in resolving the matter. Accepting responsibility for doing wrong is the first step to freedom from the wrongful situation. It may even involve a third party, like a mediator.

The model below, as outlined by Dr Ponton, provides the necessary steps to follow:

- *Acknowledge your own inner pain.* I agree that it is difficult to forgive someone without recognising the pain that it has caused you and how it has made you feel. In giving space to these feelings, it would be easier to deal with forgiveness and letting go of the pain.
- *Express those emotions in non-hurtful ways without yelling or attacking.* When someone does me an injustice and I feel hurt by those actions, the natural reaction is to defend myself. However, in a spirit of Christ-likeness, there is room for talking and working things out in a peaceable way. I would admit that this is not easy, but with Christ, all things are possible for reconciliation to take place.
- *Protect yourself from further victimisation.* Avoiding further pain and hurt, says Dr Ponton, is a wise way of not subjecting yourself to further hurt and pain by that individual/s.
- *Replace anger with compassion and learn to forgive ourselves as well.* Dr Ponton also suggested the method of understanding the

other person's point of view and what led them to behave
in the way they did. The reaction of showing compassion
was advocated by her to be a way of appeasing the situation
towards an amicable solution.

One day during a discussion with some friends, we had a
conversation on the topic of what they believe. I asked them if they
had been involved in a church before. One of them said that she was
christened as a child, and the other said that she has had nothing
to do with the church except to know of someone who goes to Mass
every day.

They both said they didn't believe because of all the evil in the
world and felt that someone was responsible for this happening and
because of things that had happened in their own lives. They found
it difficult to forgive others and admitted that they had wasted many
years with an unforgiving attitude. I shared with them the fact that
love can help us to forgive.

The gift of forgiveness provides room for growth despite the wrongs
that others do to us in life. There is a need to intentionally dismiss past
hurts and accept that we ourselves have been forgiven. Once forgiven,
I can forgive myself and let go of the pain and allow peace to take
control. The memories which may not be easy to eradicate may be
exchanged for freedom from the pain of past injustices.

9

FRIENDSHIPS

A man who has friends must himself be friendly, but
there is a friend who sticks closer than a brother.
Proverbs 18:24

W hat do you consider to be meaningful friendships that make
a difference to your life?

Alice Walker, an African American poet and writer of many books
including *The Colour Purple*, considered that no good friend would deny
you the right to speak or to grow and develop. This is fundamental
and is inherent in all of us as social beings.

If we are fortunate enough to have many friends, it gives a special
satisfaction for companionship. The world is full of lonely people,
and if you want to be a friend, you have to display the quality of
friendliness, which acts like a magnet in drawing others to you.
Friends who are true and dependable are those who will support and
provide unconditional love, regardless of the situation. They will also
find an easy and honest way to tell you the truth even if it hurts to hear
it. Somehow, you know that it's coming from a heart of love.

The gift of true friendship is wholesome and full of happiness. A
good friend fulfils the need to have someone around you that provides
camaraderie and social interaction. Yet King Solomon, known for his

wisdom, said that there is a danger in having too many friends, which might lead to a disastrous relationship.

The test of a good friend is discovered through a mutual understanding that is without selfish motives of what you can get out of the relationship. It is based on what can be shared. Our Maker did not intend for us to be alone. It is an essential component as part of the human race. Research claims that loneliness has the same effect on our mortality as smoking fifteen cigarettes a day (Crosswalk.com).

I consider a healthy friendship to be one that enables motivation and encouragement to flourish and would survive good times as well as difficult seasons. The healthy aspect is important as friends can be beneficial for mutual support and happiness.

Having prayed, I recognised the wisdom of my mother's advice, and although at times unwise choices have resulted in unpleasant outcomes for me, I still find the gift of friendships to be based on mutual respect and quality rather than quantity.

There are those who are considered fair-weather friends who are ready to abandon you when things go wrong or when there is a disagreement or difference of opinion that drives a wedge between you. This is a tough season to get through as trying to change others is futile, and you come to realise that the only person that needs changing is you!

The rich blessing that comes from good friends indicate that it is more important to develop lasting friendships with those who are not interested in your silence but want to see you grow, as Alice Walker puts it. This goes beyond the virtual friends that we find on social media.

Family members can be great friends too, as I have found in my siblings. They have been consistent in their love and togetherness as we have shared many experiences, joys, and sorrows with one another while growing up together as a close-knit family. Those fun times have lasted into adulthood. We still experience times of laughter and sharing memories that have sustained us through the rough times as well as times of celebration as we have grown together through shared love and friendships. The sense of family bonding has led us to be supportive of each other.

The test of a good friend is usually measured in this way. Their commitment means that they will remain loyal regardless and accept you for who you are. The home becomes a character-building sanctuary where you learn to appreciate good friends who never condemn you for the imperfections they see in you. They prefer to get to know you, and the relationship is one of trust.

One evening while relaxing from a hard day's work, the phone rang. It was from one of my friends, Barbara, who had been admitted to hospital. Barbara called me from the ward and asked me to come and visit her in her distressed state. She had been a colleague and friend who was going through a difficult season in her life, with her health as well as the breakdown of her marriage which had happened suddenly. Barbara lacked support from her family and called on me to come and give her the security of someone who had been a friend for some time. I immediately made myself ready and drove to the hospital and sat by her side.

As we talked, I realised how much she had been hurting, more from the loss of her relationship with her husband who had walked out on her than the physical and emotional pain she was in. She wanted to talk as she felt devastated by the way she had been treated during the relatively short time that her marriage lasted. Her family had deserted her, which had compounded the issue of needing a friend to talk to.

While we spent time together, I remembered an interesting article I once read, 'The 8 Surprising Health Benefits of Love' by Amanda Greene. In her article, she itemised the benefits of love which improves, amongst other things, improvement of the immune system and helping to live longer. Barbara was interested in this article as I shared it with her and agreed that the lack of love and friendships in our lives can cause us to feel desperate. This was her experience to the point of wanting to take her own life because of loneliness and the feeling of rejection by her family. They had pushed her away and failed to lift her up instead of letting her down.

The gift of friendships is freely given to us to share as we all deserve to be loved. Barbara and I continued to share some special moments during her hospital stay, and each time, I was able to linger until visiting time was over. I made the promise that I would return and make regular visits. Her face lit up with an unforgettable smile that warmed my heart. In my haste to see her, I did not have the time to buy flowers, but she understood as she unwrapped the gift of friendship, which meant much more to Barbara.

It is reassuring to know that the gift of friendship that Jesus offers is authentic and provides a sense of security and fellowship that outweighs all other friendships. Jesus said that He no longer calls us servants but friends. He continued to say that a servant does not know the plans of the master, but He has shared His plans with us. He accepts us, and His love shows respect for our individuality. Of course, not all friendly relationships work out, but the gift of true friendship is based on the following qualities:

Sincerity

A biblical account is given of the experience of a very wealthy man named Job. He lived in the land of Uz. Job was recognised to be 'blameless and upright' (Job 1:1). He had a reverential fear of God. He was a great role model for his children, for whom he constantly prayed. He had some friends, and the story unfolds as to the sincerity of these friends.

Job's three friends were named Eliphaz, Bildad, and Zophar. They came to see Job when they heard of the suffering he was going through. Initially, their intentions were good. When they saw Job and could not recognise him, they began to cry. They tore their robes and sprinkled dust on their heads toward heaven (Job 2:12).

Job became struck with a disease (boils) that covered his whole body. His wife had suggested that he should 'curse God and die' (Job 2:9), to which Job refused. His temptations became so severe that he became depressed and regretted being born.

The first response to sit and mourn with Job in silence would seem to be a sympathetic way for a friend to respond to a struggle where the gift of presence is valuable. There are times when no words can pacify or console, but this type of empathy is to their credit.

Their reputation as 'Job's comforters' has been regarded as insincere friendship. They began to misinterpret Job's sufferings as the consequence of sin in his life, which was not the case. Their criticism, condemnation, and insensitivity for what Job was going through must have been a blow to Job, who experienced a time of extraordinary testing with amazing patience and fortitude. Today we refer to 'the patience of Job' as an unwavering faith that waits patiently for answers and a breakthrough for circumstances to change. In the end, Job declared, 'For I know that my Redeemer lives (Job 19:25).

There are many friends like Job's friends who will make incorrect assumptions based on what their idea of suffering is and the reason why someone would be suffering as Job did. God, on the other hand, permitted Job's suffering to prove that God can protect us in the worst of circumstances.

Job was described as blameless in God's eyes, because he had an unwavering faith in God that did not shift through changes in circumstances in his life. His character remained intact, although he suffered periods of questioning God as to why He would allow it to happen to him. Like my friend, Barbara, he wanted to die. He was persecuted when Satan accused God of shielding him from pain and disaster, accusing God of giving him special protection. Job was a faithful and loyal man.

There is a happy ending to this story because Job was reinstated with all that he had before, and the end of the chapter of Job says that the Lord gave him twice as much as he had before (Job 42:10). He was then blessed with seven sons and three daughters and '14,000 sheep, 6,000 camels, 1,000 yoke of oxen, 1,000 female donkeys' (Job 42:12).

Loyalty/Commitment

Loyalty plays a huge part in maintaining a good, friendly, and lasting relationship with someone. It means not giving up on someone. It may happen when you feel that you have moved on and no longer recognise the friendship you once had, or it can be at a time when other friends take their place and, sadly, you no longer feel that the friendship holds the same value. It may also be a time when you have turned different corners and the season for that friendship has passed.

There are two biblical characters, Jonathan and David, who shared a friendship that was based on kindness, loyalty, and commitment. It involved sharing, as Jonathan shared his robe, his armour, his sword, his bow, and his belt so that David was able to go into battle against the Philistines and won, much to the anger of Jonathan's father, King Saul, as the people hailed David as victorious over the enemies as the women's chorus was, 'Saul has slain his thousands, and David his ten thousands' (1 Samuel 18:7).

This is a great example of having the gift of friendship like the comradeship that David shared with his friend Jonathan. They shared a bond that was described to be one where a covenant was made between them as a sign of their loyalty and commitment to each other (1 Samuel 18).

As best friends. Jonathan was prepared to protect David against the schemes of his father, who had become insanely jealous at David's victories that happened one after the other. Friendship sometimes involves providing protection and looking out for the other person to secure and solidify a meaningful and lasting friendship.

Mutual Support

Being there for each other and giving mutual support can make a difference to the relationship you have with friends. Good friendships take time to develop as we know and is built on trust. It is a valuable gift to treasure with the recognition that we all need the companionship of good and loyal friends for mutual support.

I have enjoyed a long-standing friendship with a colleague of mine named Yasmine. I got to know Yasmine as we were working in the same department, but in different roles. It began during a particularly stressful day that I had in the office. During this time, I was working for a manager who was verbally abusive. When I needed support from a fellow colleague, Yasmine stepped in, having witnessed her shouting on occasions, and gave me friendly support. Out of that situation, our friendship grew, and over the years, Yasmine and I have shared many work-related issues and motivated each other to overcome challenges at work as well as in our private lives.

At the time of these unpleasant incidents with the manager, I prayed about the situation and asked God to give me the kind of perseverance that I needed in this dysfunctional working relationship that had developed between the manager and me. I began to dread going into work and the expectation that each day would be the same as the day before. It began to impact on my level of job satisfaction.

The time came when, to my relief, my boss decided to resign. I hasten to add that it was not before she realised the negative effect that her style of leadership had on me and others and one day apologised to me, with a gift of chocolates. I knew that God had answered my prayer.

The gift of a good friend in need is truly a friend indeed. There has been a mutual respect between us as Yasmine is a Muslim. Our friendship defies differences in our faith, and we communicate with love, acceptance, and laughter every time we meet.

It was not surprising, therefore, when I asked Yasmine to join me for a day at a London theatre, a gift for Mother's Day from my children, that she readily accepted. Like all other times, we shared all the things that we needed to share, and it was truly a memorable event as we sat and had lunch together and then went on to the show that was lively and entertaining.

Throughout these and other times, God gave me many work colleagues who became friends, with whom we could share and solve problems together, which has been an enriching experience over the years.

The gift of friendships has become a supportive communication tool through work challenges, with the element of trust and loyalty that is expected of a true friend. The aspect of sincerity is found in a friend who is there during the down times and can help to encourage the other person in achieving goals and overcoming setbacks.

The strong foundation is built through a grounded understanding of each other and a consistent feeling of mutual support, even if there is a gap in communication, and being able to pick up from there, which Yasmine and I call 'catching up' time.

While reflecting on our friendship, Yasmine shared qualities that keep our friendship strong and lasting, such as kindness, trust, and loyalty, which we both appreciate as important in maintaining a long-lasting friendship.

The aspect of being able to laugh and have a sense of humour is a special gift for both of us, along with the 'incredible work ethic', which she said she has recognised in me. It has taught her that even at times when you don't get what you want, if you continue to be yourself and improve on your work style, it becomes a special friendship.

We know that friends come into our lives sometimes for a specific purpose and season. The ability to remain constant and reliable is the basis for a good friendship, when you became a sounding board for each other and a confidant at times, when you need someone whom you can entrust your innermost thoughts and feelings.

The quality of friendship that Jesus offers is consistent with His character and based on love, consistency, acceptance, and commitment. Just as Jonathan shared everything with his friend David, Jesus extends His hand of friendship that brings happiness and contentment. This is an incredible gift.

10

GRATITUDE

Blessed be the Lord who daily loads us with
benefits, the God of our Salvation.
Psalm 68:19

What are you thankful for, and what is it about the gift of gratitude that helps you to maintain a sense of thanksgiving for what you have?

Gratitude is said to be the gateway to increase so that the more gratitude is expressed, the more blessings flow through the channels of thanksgiving. The gift of thankfulness helps to bring healing during times of sickness and helps to give me a different perspective by shifting my thoughts from whatever season I am going through to feeling blessed despite whatever setbacks there may be.

Gratitude emanates from a heart of thankfulness for the small and great things that are part of daily life, as God pours His love upon us in different ways. It means having an appreciation for what you have and being grateful. Things have a way of changing when gratitude is expressed, because it changes my altitude and attitude. It also stops me from taking things or people for granted.

The start of a new day is a reason for gratitude and thanksgiving because of the blessings and daily benefits it brings that are worthy of gratitude. This is a gift that is linked in with thanksgiving and recognition for all the blessings that are received.

> The sense of gratitude comes from the contentment of having those around who care and are interested in the well-being of others. The invitation to accept spiritual gifts like the fruit of the Holy Spirit can bring a sense of connection to the Almighty who knows and is always there to supply needs.

People and situations may try to hinder giving praises to God, but we are encouraged to serve and praise Him, irrespective of the season. We then become unstoppable. I love reading the book of Psalms as it is one of my favourites, although there are so many. It is where the psalmist David announced that continual praise would always be an expression of gratefulness to God.

I therefore give thanks for the way I am led to redirect my thinking, and a sense of contentment highlights so many things I can be thankful for! I can also be thankful for people I can call or who call me at the right time to offer ideas that work out to be creative in helping me to feel better about a particular situation.

I give thanks that at all times I am totally dependent on Him and know that relying on God is my only option to bring me out into a state of well-being. Having a positive attitude, especially at times of unemployment when I needed God's provision, prevented negative feelings. Yet lurking behind all that was an opportunity to see that I have everything to thank Him for as I 'give thanks to the Lord for He is good' (Psalm 136:1).

Thanking God as you weather the seasonal storms, be it sunshine or rain, acknowledges how little control we have over these things sometimes. In preserving our lives, there is a recognition of our need of Him in the small blessings as well as the big ones. We become indebted to Him for being true to His Word and for shielding us from harm even when unaware of His presence to help. He satisfies the need for a grateful heart and assumes the fatherly role of love and support. The Bible tells us that He gives us everything we need in due season.

There is always a time to be grateful for God's indescribable love, mercy, and compassion and His saving grace. His faithfulness and ever-present help in trouble is worthy of trust, and His healing power, whether on a spiritual or physical level, is cause for rejoicing.

There was an occasion when Jesus travelled through Samaria and Galilee. As He arrived in one of the villages, there were ten men who had leprosy and as such were classed as outcasts in the community because of their dreaded and incurable disease. The gravity of their situation caused them to naturally cry for help from the only One who could heal them of their disease.

Of all diseases known in the East the leprosy was most dreaded (EG White, Desire of Ages).

As Jesus entered the village, these ten men knew this was their only opportunity to plead for His merciful touch of healing and cleansing. Their voices were intense as 'they lifted up their voices and said Jesus, Master, have mercy on us' (Luke 17:13). They all needed healing, a condition which put them on a level playing field, regardless of any cultural differences they may have had.

Jesus observed the custom of the day and responded by giving them the command to go and show themselves to the priest. Without hesitation, they went in obedience and, in doing so, were cleansed of their leprous condition.

They could now return to their homes and families, having been made completely healed, and were welcomed back into society. Their season of change began when they spoke the words "have mercy on us". It would be realistic to expect that a miracle of such magnitude would warrant gratitude at the highest level and that they would all return with excitement and gratefulness to show appreciation for what Jesus had done in cleansing and making them whole. Sadly, only one remembered to give thanks and show gratitude for what Jesus had done in curing their disease.

Only one returned to say thank you, to which Jesus asked, 'Were there not ten cleansed? But where are the nine?' (Luke 17:17).

Praise is second nature to those who trust in God because Psalm 33:1 says: 'Rejoice in the Lord, O you righteous! for praise from the upright is beautiful.' It is at the time when I think I have least to rejoice about that I count my blessings and find it surprising that there is more to thank Him for than I had thought. At times, my gratitude journal reminds me that there are so many things that are likely to be forgotten if I didn't occasionally reflect on them.

Contentment that is experienced through gratitude reveals God's benevolent nature because it is so easy to forget, like the nine leapers who went their way and forgot to turn back and express gratitude for their healing from leprosy. I need the act of gratitude that translates into contentment and joy.

11

GOD'S LOVE

> If every computer in the world was used to describe the love of
> God, and every database and internet website was filled; and
> the skies were simply made up of paper to write on from one
> end of the world to the next, and every tree became a pen, and
> we were all computer operators assigned to write about the love
> of God, we still would not be able to adequately describe it.
> *Unknown*

How has love made a difference to your life? The gift of God's
love is the greatest gift of all!

It was Friday, the day we know as Good Friday. It was far from
a good day for Jesus as He stepped into His Father's will on behalf
of all of humanity. In His final moments before the cross, He had
prayed for an escape from this ordeal but knew that it was the only
way. Nevertheless, He accepted God's Will.

The prospect of going to the cross was the purpose for which He
came, but now in those final hours in Gethsemane, He identified with
the pain, agony, loss, and loneliness that typify human existence.

It must have felt like the longest day in history, as Jesus experienced
separation from the Father and denial by one of his closest friends,
Peter, whom He knew would cave in under the weight of the pressure
to deny that he knew Jesus. Jesus told him that this would happen, but

he did not want to believe it. He was not strong enough or prepared enough for the trial of defending His Lord at a time when it mattered most. The betrayal of Judas was nothing of a surprise either, whose kiss was the kiss of death to satisfy Jesus's enemies, now about to take hold of Him for an imminent death on a cruel cross.

Jesus was taken along the Via Dolorosa, otherwise known as the sorrowful way, a traditional path that led to the place of the crucifixion, called Mount Calvary. This journey must have been long for someone who was paying the price for a sin He did not commit. It was a road strewn with sorrow and grief for me. He had travelled many roads with His disciples and followers during His ministry, but this was the only road that He could travel on His own, as the greatest gift of all. His sacrificial love would now be painstakingly poured out with His own blood.

The noise of the crowds must have been deafening as they chanted the words 'Crucify Him! Crucify Him!' What did He do except to bring healing and restoration to so many and changed sorrow into healing and death to life? He gave hope to millions, revolutionised lives, filled the cups of empty people, and treated those hurting and marginalised with respect and restored their dignity. He taught the golden rule which invites all people to be treated with equality as He broke the barriers of segregation and treated people with forgiveness and respect. The love of God is the greatest gift because it satisfies the human need for unconditional love. It surpasses all other loves and comes from the heart of a loving Heavenly Father. His love is universally extended to everyone, 'For God so loved the world that He gave His only begotten Son that whoever believes in Him should not perish but have eternal life' (John 3:16). The love of God is endless and unites everyone with peace, love, and acceptance.

The incredible gift of God's love is shown in Jesus's willingness to sacrifice His life to restore the original relationship God had with His creation. I respond to this incredible love by accepting the gift for myself and realising that He faced and endured the cross for me.

The nails that fastened Him to the cross would forever be the final price for my sin and the sin of the entire world. The burden was great but nevertheless, he accepted God's Will in submission. I am so glad that Jesus went through with it in obedience and provides an example for me when I am faced with difficult seasons that I do not want to experience.

I rejoice in the fact that after Good Friday came the day of His resurrection the following Sunday. The promise was fulfilled. His love is a gift worth claiming and has become the greatest gift of all! It surpasses all other gifts. The cross therefore represents the 'fullest extent of God's love and sacrifice as He took on the penalty for sin for the world', says Jack Sequeira, author of *Beyond Belief.*

God's love influenced my thinking in terms of how to give love without expecting love in return. From God's example, I learned that love makes all the difference when confronted with hostility and confrontation. It accepts others as they are without trying to change anyone.

It conquers and removes mountains and melts the coldest heart. Jesus used love to heal and restore people and is the example I want to follow. No other love its match can find. It is all-encompassing and is a perfect gift from a Father who, unlike humankind, shows 'no variation or shadow of turning' (James 1:17).

One of the ways that reassures me that His love is the greatest love of all is that it is immeasurable and unconditional. As it is unconditional, I do not have to be perfect before He loves me. I just need to willingly accept His love, which offers freedom and the power to restore brokenness and melt the hardest heart through conversion.

I recall how God showed His love by protecting me from a potential accident one day. It happened four years ago when I knew that my old car was coming to the end of its life. It had surprisingly passed its MOT (Ministry of Transport) certificate, which I considered to be a miracle. I loved my old car and had become so familiar and comfortable with it that I kept holding on to it and spending lots of money to get parts replaced. The day finally came during a journey back from church when my cherished car finally decided it could not carry me anymore! It had broken down within a short distance from my home, and I was very thankful that it did not happen while I was travelling on the motorway.

I had reached a dual carriageway where the car finally came to a halt, but it was not a danger to me or other road users. When the emergency service came, the car was towed away. I marvelled at how good God is and how His love and protection was experienced in a practical way that day. He also provided me with a new car, which I had been praying for as I now needed a reliable vehicle for travelling to work.

God's love is extended to me through my thought processes, frustration with waiting, doubting, failure to trust God implicitly, and so on. At these times, I need to rely on the greatest gift of all, His love, to sustain me throughout the day.

The love of God makes a difference in my life because it has given me a perfect example of how it is possible to love Him, others, and myself. He will not disappoint me or let me down, like my old car. In the reality of my own imperfection, it is knowing that His love is a perfect gift. It gives me reassurance that I can rely on Him. It gives a sense of gratitude for His undeserved love. I do not need to impress God because He knows me fully anyway, so I can relax in His love.

His gift of love is the greatest as no one can ever replicate the value of such love. There is no other person who can fill the emptiness inside for wholesomeness. It surpasses any other love that a human being is capable of expressing.

Getting to know God's love is a lifetime journey for me. It is a transparent love that wants only the best for His children, who love Him in return. I want to love Him more and return it in some measure, but even in this desire, He is willing to help me to reach that place, so I need Him.

His care is evidenced through creation and also through answered prayers, problems that have been resolved, and moments of healing. I depend on Him for every provision, and He supplies my needs. These can sometimes be seemingly simple ways, and at other times, it is on a much-bigger scale.

The daily journey in life that I encounter has no comparison to the perfect life that Jesus lived. The daily challenges that I experience bears no resemblance to what He suffered on the cross of Calvary. No act of submission on my part equates to the submission Jesus endured. His love is a gift that is extended in a way that I can understand and appreciate. The cross was His day of triumph as He cried out that His mission was completed.

God's love is all-encompassing that takes in everything I have ever done or will do in the future. There are many ways that prove God's love for me. Knowing that I am one of His children and that He welcomes me just as I am as a member of His family makes me feel loved and secure. I feel His love when He provides for my needs or protects and surrounds me with assurances and blessings. I feel His love when I come to Him in prayer and sense His presence and forgiveness even though I am tempted to doubt Him sometimes in the confusion of life's seasons.

12

HEALING

We squander our health in search of wealth.
Pearce

Through healing, the centurion had no doubt whatsoever that Jesus could perform a miracle of healing and recognised that distance made no difference to Jesus. He just had to say the word, and it would be done, just like his own experience as a ruler, but he did not have the power to heal someone

Many might attest to the fact that we sometimes trade our health for wealth. We put our health on hold, hoping to pay attention to it when we are a lot older or when sickness comes. Yet a healthy life is irreplaceable by any other thing that brings temporary gratification because prevention makes for unwarranted cure.

The need to be health-conscious is becoming more and more a number one priority for many who find it to relieve stress levels, as wisely spoken by Mahatma Gandhi, who said that our health is our real wealth. As we know, living a healthy lifestyle is central to longevity and the quality of wellness that meets the needs of all. Therefore, the gift of health cannot be equalled to any other priority that will one day be left behind, because the fact is that we cannot take anything with us when we die.

There are many benefits to a good, healthy lifestyle that leads to healing. Now more than ever, a strong emphasis is placed on healthy diets, exercise, and alternative meat-free foods like a vegetarian or vegan diet. At the present time, there are television programmes that focus on healthy meals, and a variety of cookbooks bring an assortment of choices for maintaining good, healthy living practices.

I was introduced to vegetarianism when I made my decision to try vegetarian dishes because of the benefits of a healthier diet. It has been a journey of trying out new dishes and learning how to prepare foods without the use of meat. This was initially a challenge. I then was amazed to find that there are so many interesting dishes that can be prepared that are both healthy and satisfying. As with all life changes, the process is gradual and includes the choice to change from meat-eating to a total vegetarian diet.

Jan Arkless, author of *No Meat for Me Please!* recommended vegetarian dishes to non-vegetarians who were persuaded to try some of the delicious real vegetarian dishes, and many were pleasantly surprised. She said that anyone who did not like nut roast would try it and, eventually, after persuasion, would enjoy the pleasant and healthy alternative option to meat.

For many years, I enjoyed a regular personal fitness programme, and this helped me to maintain a good life balance of work and recreation. It has had the added benefit of socialising and making friends with regular gym club members when I visited the local gym for my weekly swim.

Exercise also has the benefit of being a great mood elevator. It has contributed to a happy state of striving for a healthy way of life and enjoying the pleasure of looking and feeling good as I grow older. When everything functions well, longevity of life is a treasured gift.

Despite all the above efforts to live a healthy life, the changing seasons of life interrupt this way of life that can cause you to stop and think about the consequence of wrong choices. The rest and relaxation during holidays, away from the day-to-day activities, spending quality time with family and friends, provide a well-earned break that is refreshing and therapeutic.

Many years ago, before my mother died, she developed type 2 diabetes, and I do not recall her suffering from major complications from the disease. She managed it well, and whilst I had some general knowledge of diabetes as I watched her manage the condition, I had a limited understanding of the disease and how it could be healed.

I was encouraged by my mother's faith and observed how she was able to cope with the diagnosis without becoming stressed or overly anxious about it. She exercised contentment and had the strong belief that despite her health challenges, she could still unwrap the gift of healing and well-being. She maintained at the time that by doing so, if we do our best, God will do the rest. Yet I hoped that I might escape this illness, although I realised that I was predisposed to it now that it affected my mother.

The gift of healing has been an ongoing and challenging battle for me, where I have accepted and depended on God for guidance and protection. He has been faithful in supporting me when I found myself in desperate need of his healing during my diabetic journey. On occasions when I experienced glycaemic episodes, I was somewhere where I was able to get assistance and was protected from danger.

The apostle, Paul, prayed for healing so that a thorn he had could be removed but was assured that God's grace was always sufficient. In my case, diabetes has been the thorn from which I have prayed to be healed in order to experience total recovery. Over the last twenty years or more, I have managed to avoid becoming insulin-dependent, which was an early prediction.

Along the path of healing and cooperating with the advice and guidance of professional doctors and those who are qualified to provide medical intervention, there are some self-help remedies that can be taken to enrich life and promote a healthy lifestyle, while waiting for the season to change.

Some of these I have experienced to be helpful:

- *Nutritional foods.* It's easier to settle for quick, fast foods than to organise the week's meal plan ahead of time. I had a dietician who helped me to 'weed out' the unhelpful options that were part of my daily lunches and snacks. I then had the option to look at labels more and detect the hidden sugars in foods that I enjoyed but now had to avoid.
- *Endurance and perseverance.* These help to reach goals. It is difficult to reach goals when you are faced with what seems

like an impossible task. The need to take a day at a time can help to provide a good level of contentment and perseverance, especially when you cannot see the results straight away. It is like trying to climb a mountain all in one day. It takes a bite-sized attitude to the problem and reassure yourself that you will get there eventually.

- *Wellness planning.* This was a challenge as it not only involved regular exercise but also required the need to destress and develop a can-do attitude. I had to reinforce the thought that I could manage diabetes instead of allowing it to manage me.
- *Sharing experiences with others as a learning platform.*
- *Temperance.* This involves moderation and maintaining a healthy balance which includes planning and organisation with avoidance of harmful substances.
- *Ask God what His will is in this situation.* There is a purpose in everything, and nothing happens by chance. It may be a time of gaining a better understanding of His resources and how trusting in Him can be the breakthrough that is needed.
- *Recognise your value.* There's the 'Why me?' feeling that comes when going through a particular season of disappointment through ill health. It became overwhelming for me to get beyond the feeling that if it has been done for someone else, it can be done for me. Sickness has a way of challenging that low feeling that you don't matter to God, but in reality, you do. It's holding on to that knowledge that helps me rise above the failure, to recognise my value with reassurance that God knows my need for healing.
- *Total reliance on God.* In the quest for a new start, total reliance on God is key. The reliance comes through prayer and asking for His guidance so that the changes can be sustainable in striving for the gift of good health.

My daily prayer is that God's gift of healing, assisted by a healthy lifestyle, would be sufficient to supply a sense of well-being, granting vigour and strength to transform our days. Through His power, He can make us into whole persons when sickness has threatened our ability to be in perfect health and harmony with His will.

Abraham lived to the very old age of 175 years old (Genesis 25:7). Whether or not our lifespan goes beyond the allotted time span, the plan for healing was the original design as a gift from the Creator, as He healed so many who were blind, crippled, diseased and suffering from mental health.

> Every season has its purpose. Experiencing restoration and peace of mind is granted through the gift of healing so that the process becomes one of abundance of love being poured out every day.
>
> When faced with sickness, prayer and giving the matter over to God bring peace, which in turn may affect His healing within His will. It requires trusting Him to carry you through this challenging season. Our level of responsibility is to maintain a good, healthy regime that would ward off avoidable disease and pain, whatever the period in which you find yourself.

The gift of healing may not always be instantaneous. The healing continues. It is dependent on faith and patience that the healing will come. There may be many layers to unwrap to discover the root causes and to overcome. The reliance on His promise to prosper in all things, regardless of the season, is given in the assurance of good health, even as our soul prospers (3 John 1:2).

The story of the healing of the centurion's servant mentioned earlier brings consolation that God can heal.

13

HOPE

Hope is a belief in an expected outcome related
to events and circumstances in one's life.
Unknown

What is your understanding of living a life of hope, and how has
the gift helped you to surmount a particular challenge in your life?

Hope is a gift that provides a foundation for living a contented life.
It comes when you believe that God can be trusted to take you through
whatever season you are in. When things happen, it is hope that keeps
us holding on to a greater good and purpose. Hope is the fuel that
renews my belief that God is as close as I would want Him to be.

An experience of the gift of hope occurred in a village in Palestine
called Emmaus, within a thirty-kilometre distance from Jerusalem.
There were two of Jesus's disciples who walked along the Emmaus
road together. They shared the end of their hopes that had been
shattered. One of them was called Cleopas. As they travelled along,
their hearts and heads were bowed low because of the death of their
Saviour, Jesus Christ. He had been crucified, and His death, in their
estimation, was the end of their journey with Him as their Leader.

There was a feeling of helplessness and hopelessness as they
recounted the tremendous impact Jesus would have made to their
future deliverance from Israel. They expressed the hope that He would

have been the one to rescue and redeem them (Luke 24:21). Now He was crucified and worse still, the tomb was empty. He had been taken away from them. They were distraught and deeply disappointed. They could not imagine life without Him.

They had lost their beloved Leader, and a bleak future now lay ahead of them, as they consoled each other on the journey, with the memories of what could have been. During Jesus's ministry, walking, talking, and learning from the Master must have been the most joyous experience they had ever experienced in their lives and upon which their hopes were built. He was the rope they had clung to and the lifeline that kept the disciples together.

While they were at their lowest point of despair, a 'stranger' joined them and listened to their conversation. He wanted to know what they were talking about and why they were so sad. Cleopas and his fellow disciple were surprised that the stranger was not aware of all that had been happening about Jesus's crucifixion. He seemed to be the only one who was unaware of the crucifixion!

Jesus began to share God's purpose in what had happened on the cross and began to talk to them about what Moses and all the other prophets had said that pointed to His death, which was a fulfilment of Scripture. He gave them a Bible lesson that focused not on what had happened but on what God said would happen.

At the end of their travel, they begged the stranger to stay with them, and they had a meal together. It was only at this point when Jesus broke the bread and blessed it, that they recognised that it was Jesus all along! When He left them, they reflected and confessed, 'Did not our heart burn within us while He talked with us on the road, and while He opened the Scriptures to us?' Through renewed courage, they were able to use the gift of hope and discernment by walking with Jesus (Luke 24:32).

You may be going through a season in your life when you think you have lost hope feeling all alone, and when nothing seems to be going right. Disappointment and despair set in, and you feel disillusioned with life. You are not alone. This was the experience of two of Jesus's followers after His death as they travelled along the Emmaus road. Heads bowed and hearts low, they felt let down, and hope was nowhere in sight.

Jesus's death on the cross was not the end of the story but the beginning. When our hope is built on Jesus Christ, He becomes our solid rock that is anchored on the security of His promise of life after death. Hope becomes the basis of an expected outcome. The roadblocks on the journey become steppingstones to a better future.

The disciples' hope had a direct correlation to what they were going through. Hope kept them connected and would be the key to their survival from now on. Sometimes when going through difficult moments of trials and temptations, it's easy to think that there is no one who can come alongside us who knows and understands our hurts. It is at these times that He draws close to encourage us that He knows and is at the centre of what we are going through. Ella Wheeler Wilcox, a renowned poet, considered hope to be the set of sails and not the gales that charters our course in life.

When things look gloomy through setbacks, the best source is to go back to the Bible and find out what God said. Reading about His promise to keep and protect will dispel the doubts and keep our hopes vibrant. Their hope was that Jesus would redeem Israel. Little did they know that He is the Redeemer and is the only one who could 'redeem Israel', but not in the way they thought.

When people are taken away from us through separation by death, it brings a sense of hopelessness as the memory brings immeasurable sadness and grief. Many people who have lost their loved one through killings and crimes will always recount on the hopes they had for a young man or woman whose life was prematurely and needlessly taken away from them. They speak of the great tragedy and the potential they had and their huge sadness of losing a life. It was the hope they had of someone who would have made a huge difference to their world.

One inspiring story of hope is illustrated by the experience of a man named George Mueller, a nineteenth-century Christian evangelist and missionary who opened up orphanages in England for homeless girls. He had little or no money, only faith and hope that he could achieve the work of providing homes for homeless girls on the streets. All he had was hope that allowed him to defy all the odds for those young girls who were helpless and vulnerable.

His sense of hope led him to show compassion to those most in need of it and to extend a helping hand to those who could not help themselves. From just a couple of girls, there were amongst 300 children who eventually were provided with accommodation and food as his venture began to expand, bringing hope to the hopeless.

The story unfolds that on one occasion, George Mueller told the 300 girls to sit at the table, knowing that there was no food to give them. He prayed, and with thanksgiving, he waited for God to provide food for these hungry girls. Not long after his prayer, there was a knock on the door, and a baker told George that after a sleepless night, he decided to get up early and bake three batches of loaves for him.

Following that, a milkman knocked and said that his cart had broken down and that all his milk would likely be spoilt by the time the cart was taken to the garage to be fixed. He asked whether George could use the milk, free of charge. George graciously accepted his kind offer and thanked God for answered prayers. The story ends with, 'It was just enough for 300 thirsty children.'

I experienced hope at the beginning of the global pandemic in 2020. I was laid off and was out of work for a short period. I was told that my role within the team was ended. This happened very abruptly. Many were redeployed during this time of lockdown or given the opportunity to work from home. The possibility of getting another job seemed daunting at this point.

When I received the news that the job had suddenly ended, I was devastated. I began to pray for God to open up another door to allow me to earn a living again. I then placed my hope in some other opportunity, and the job search began yet again. I contacted many agencies I was registered with on previous occasions, but nothing materialised. I decided not to lose hope and kept surfing the internet. The chances of employment were slim at that time with unemployment figures rising due to the pandemic.

The day finally came during a search on the employee online website. I saw a vacancy that was advertised within a team that I had worked in previously to cover for maternity leave. It was now advertised as a permanent position. The closing date was within a few days, so I had to submit my application straight away, hoping that I would be selected for interview. Shortly after submitting my application, I was selected for interview and was pleased after the interview to be offered a permanent job. It came at just the right time.

It was amazing to see how God's provision made it possible through hope and prayer. Hope has a way of bringing results and works alongside faith. It is also a time to be active while waiting for answers to prayer.

My strategy for coping whenever I fail to unwrap the gift of hope is to remember that belief makes everything possible, as in the case of George Mueller, who defied the odds and produced a good outcome through hope.

The means by which it is possible to live a contentment-centred life gives hope for the future, knowing that although it is not possible to change some things as they may be beyond our control, the One who holds the future gives hope for tomorrow. He wants to imbue us with hope and a future despite all that is happening to suggest otherwise.

Through the gift of hope, there is an expectation of a better day. It was time to set my sails so that the gales of life would not overturn my hope and charter a better future.

Like faith, hope is a way of overcoming obstacles as I learn to appreciate that life is really what you make it. Hope is strengthened through prayer. Hope seeks to believe that God will provide in a magnificent way for our needs at every stage. Launching out in expectation of His promise to remain faithful gives vivid hope, and personal commitment to Him is an important factor.

Whatever is in store for you, the gift of hope will help to accomplish it. The ability to see the other side of problems is not ours to view. The knowledge that we will be taken along the journey a day at a time will imbue me with confidence in putting hope first.

The Christian's hope is one that brings reassurance that He is with us during our darkest moments during the changing seasons of life. Faith holds on to hope. Hope holds on to re-assurance, and re-assurance links up with faith to form an invincible circle. God then turns sadness into gladness, and weakness into strength that is realistic as we hold on to the expected outcome of circumstances. We hold on even when there is nothing else left but the will to hold on.

There are five lessons that can be taken from this incident from this incident of the disciples on the Emmaus road:

1. When we think that we are walking alone, we are not. Jesus comes alongside us and brightens the journey with His presence. There is never a time that we are tempted to feel alone as it is now, with so much isolation and sadness around us.
2. While the disciples were at their lowest point of despair, Jesus joined them. Jesus knows about the pain of human suffering. He wants to lift our spirits and align us with His Will and purpose.
3. Walking with Jesus gives us hope for the future.
4. Hope keeps us holding on to a greater good out of what we are going through. It is the fuel that renews belief that God is as close as we would want Him to be. While the disciples were pondering about their loss of their loved One, Jesus came and reminded them of the Scriptures and what was being fulfilled.
5. Launching out in expectation of His promise to remain faithful keeps hope alive.

For I know the thoughts that I think toward you, says the Lord, thoughts of peace and not of evil, to give you a future and a hope. (Jeremiah 29:11)

14

HOSPITALITY

Do not forget to entertain strangers, for by so doing
some have unwittingly entertained angels.
Hebrews 13:2

How does the gift of hospitality motivate you to extend
generosity to those less fortunate than yourself?

My daily reading on this topic of hospitality came from the book
This Quiet Place, focused on creative hospitality and how it can mean so
many things. The writer, Fonda Cordis Chaffer, said that 'hospitality
can be flowers, as well as well as offering a bed to a stranger'. She
said that it can include a telephone call as well as giving a blanket to
a new baby.

Paul encouraged us to distribute 'to the needs of the saints, given
to hospitality' (Romans 12:13). This gift is therefore accessible to
everyone who courageously accepts it, given with love. For this reason,
sharing what you have can take many forms. It can simply be a way
of giving encouragement, listening and giving practical support.

Hospitality requires humility to reach out and give whatever you
have so that others can experience love, which is more important.
I believe that the Lord can use whatever little we have and turn
it into something great to make a difference through the spirit of
generosity. Sharing can sometimes involve sacrifice in giving away

things you consider precious too in order to meet the needs of someone else. Sharing can be fun. It means having an open heart and letting others in.

There is a need to recognise that I may be entertaining angels unawares and a time for listening as well as the practical aspect of preparation. Sometimes it means being brave to face rejection as there may be times when the invitation is made and the offer is not readily accepted, and you feel let down.

I can look for ways to share and show hospitality to those around me, bringing a smile and a positive attitude whenever the opportunity arises. By using my gift of creativity, I can look for ways to be of service to the community.

It can mean a simple bowl of soup to a lonely, shut-in neighbour or helping with someone's shopping during bad weather conditions. Hospitality can be shown when I am willing to ask someone questions like, what are your needs? How can I help you? Is there anything I can do to make things better for you? What is the best way I can support you? When is the best time to call you?

Hospitality can also involve listening to someone who is hurting emotionally and in desperate need of friendship and a hand to hold on to. The gift of time can be a much-needed form of support, which is something anyone can do.

During Jesus's earthly ministry, hospitality was shown to Him on an occasion when he visited the home of two friends, Mary and Martha, who lived in Bethany, east of Jerusalem. Martha is said to have been the one who welcomed Jesus into her house, showing the gift of hospitality (Luke 10:38–42).

In preparation for His visit, Martha was busily preparing a meal for their special guest, Jesus, and they both made Him feel welcome and comfortable. This is an important part of hospitality where you prepare something ahead of time, but even a drink of water is offered to the guest. Martha was extremely busy with preparation, and so she spent most of her time in the kitchen, and became exhausted in the process. She complained to Jesus that her sister had left her to do all the serving on her own.

Martha expressed her openness by complaining to Jesus because she wanted Mary to come and help her serve. Jesus told her about priorities as He recognised that she was becoming worried about it. He told her that the part that Mary had chosen was the most important one.

I often get these two mixed up. Trying to do my best for the Master is not as important as allowing Him to help me to be my best through quality time spent in His presence. After all, if Jesus could turn water into wine, surely He could have transformed a miracle if Martha needed it. She just needed to get her priorities right. I'm sure Jesus would have performed a miracle of food for them if only she had asked Him!

This is also a gift of hospitality when guests are made to feel that quality time is of equal importance alongside enjoying a well-prepared meal.

Using the opportunity to get to know the guest in a more relational way, to break the ice, and to make a compliment to them are all excellent ways of using the gift of hospitality. This changes the atmosphere to one of acceptance, and a welcoming attitude will help them to relax and enjoy the visit to your home.

The gift of hospitality can be shown in the gracious invitation to someone who you want to show appreciation to. It doesn't matter whether there is plenty or little. The blessing comes when there is sharing with someone who needs a helping hand to be extended to them even though the individual might not be someone you would naturally be drawn to or feel they are outside of your social circle.

An account in 2 Samuel 9 gives a heart-felt story of hospitality. After the death of David's best friend, Jonathan, David was now a king and was in a position to extend the gift of hospitality to Jonathan's son, Mephibosheth. He had been injured at birth and became disabled. David never forgot the special friendship he had with Jonathan and made the request as to whether there was someone of Saul's household that he could show kindness to (2 Samuel 9). They found Mephibosheth. He was brought to David's table, and the gift of hospitality was extended to him for the sake of his father, Jonathan. Mephibosheth accepted David's welcoming and kind gift that was offered to him and took his place at the king's table.

When an effort is made to go the extra mile in showing hospitality, it shows that the guest is worth the effort and gives them a feeling of being appreciated and that their company is valued, as in the case of Mary and Martha's special guest, Jesus.

The gift of hospitality is known to have a knock-on effect as the giver gains the satisfaction of reaching out and the reward is given upon seeing someone benefit from a generous spirit. The gift is unwrapped to reveal a heart of compassion in responding sensitively to needs, with the desire to entertain others.

In John 6, there is an account given when a boy demonstrated the gift of sharing his lunch. On this occasion, Jesus was on the mountain preaching to a great multitude around Him. At the end of His discourse, the disciples wanted to send the people away, but Jesus knew that this was an opportunity for Him to be glorified through a miracle of showing the gift of hospitality to the crowd. He asked the crowd to sit down. Jesus was aware of their physical needs and wanted to feed them. From the crowd came a little boy who had just five barley loaves and two small fish for his lunch. Jesus used his lunch to perform the miracle of feeding 5,000 (John 6:9).

It would have taken no less than a miracle for his lunch to serve 5,000 hungry people, but Jesus was able to perform the miracle from what was presented to Him. There was more than enough, as twelve baskets of fragments were left over. Jesus told the disciples to gather what was left so that nothing was wasted. As a result of this miracle, those who witnessed what happened said, 'This is truly the Prophet who is to come into the world' (John 6:14).

> The most important lesson of just loaves and fish was that Jesus blessed the meagre offering that the boy had, and with it, thousands were fed. The gift of hospitality exemplifies the principle of giving what little we have, which leads to innumerable blessings.

There was a culture of hospitality when I was growing up in Barbados. It didn't matter how little you had; the gift of sharing meant that there was enough to give. It was not uncommon for neighbours to have an open door and an unspoken rule where friends and their children in the community felt welcomed to walk in and play games.

I remember it was a sharing community, so neighbours often would feed other people's children if they visited and were hungry.

The concept that it takes a village to be involved in raising a child might have been the belief at that time of extending hospitality to all.

My mother was a shining example of someone who was blessed with the gift of hospitality, and sharing was second nature to her. She enjoyed the pleasure of sharing whatever she had not only to her family, but anyone who came to our home was welcome, and there was always enough love and especially delicious food to share. Our home was an open place for visitors, and she would cook enough so that there was some left over, just in case.

A spirit of plenty and a generous disposition is evidenced in the gift of hospitality. Whatever she had, she just wanted to share it. She also used it as an opportunity to share the Gospel as well.

She loved having everyone together, and the more of us were there, the happier she was. When visitors came to the home, she would bake a cake, and the only thing she would not entertain was refusal to accept it!

Having had many opportunities to receive and also show hospitality, I can attest to the fact that it is a rewarding gift that led to a life of contentment for what you have. You kept a little, shared a little, and saved a little (if you could). It can be shown to family, friends, members of the community, the lonely, work colleagues, a sick one who needs a shelter, or someone in transition from homelessness to moving into a home of their own.

The Lord can use whatever little we have and turn it into something great to feed a multitude if we are prepared to have a spirit of hospitality and generosity. The gift is motiveless, selfless, with a spirit of charitable giving, and underpinned by love. It is a gift that showcases a Heavenly Father who gives good gifts to His children, who in turn can share and receive hospitality.

15

LOVE

I have loved you with an everlasting love; therefore
with lovingkindness I have drawn you.
Jeremiah 31:3

Do you feel loved? How has this gift helped you to understand God's love?

This gift of love is for you, specially wrapped as everlasting and imperishable. We have been loved by God with a love that is endless and filled with loving-kindness. Everyone responds to love and may express it in different ways. It is by far the greatest gift that humans can experience. Love is said to be the strongest word in the vocabulary and is understood in every language and tongue as the emotional experience that makes the world go round. It defies all barriers and is a force that is transforming and radiating and gives direction and purpose to life.

We know that from birth, a baby needs love in order to thrive, and throughout adult life, giving and sharing the gift of love transforms a person. We all need love to feel warm and accepted by others. When love is truly expressed, it gives us a sense of belonging and self-worth. Nothing quite works like love. It covers everything. It melts away rejection, criticism, and failure and brings a feeling of recognition and hope.

Love is based on an intense and deep feeling or sentiment which everyone has a capacity for. We were designed in this way because God is love. There are many words to describe love, so there are varying degrees of love that is part of the human experience. Some of the many different types of love include eros (romantic), filial (platonic), and agape (divine, self-sacrificing) love.

The book of Hosea, with only fourteen chapters, is a remarkable story of the enduring gift of love. It demonstrates expressions of love, forgiveness, and compassion. Hosea was a prophet and the son of Beeri, during the reigning time of Uzziah and Hezekiah, amongst the kings of Judah. God spoke to Hosea and gave him a special message that would be similar to the way that Israel was turning their backs on Him. God loved them and wanted to show love to them through the example of Hosea's experience. It was God's love that was displayed as parallel to a husband-and-wife relationship.

God told Hosea to marry a woman of ill repute (Hosea 1:2). Her name was Gomer. This would seem an unusual request from God, but Hosea's action of obedience and trust in marrying a woman of 'great harlotry' was to be symbolic of the way that Israel had gone far away from Him and was worshipping false gods.

Hosea's family comprised his wife, Gomer, who had a son called Jezeel, and God said that his name meant that God was about to bring an end to Israel's kingdom. Gomer then had a daughter named Lo-Ruhamah, which meant God's removal of mercy from Israel. The son to follow was named Lo-Ammi, and God said, 'For you are not my people and I will not be your God' (Hosea 1:9).

Hosea's love for Gomer did not change her previous lifestyle. She still pursued other lovers. However, Hosea still loved her. He remained faithful to her even though she committed adultery. This reflects those who reject God's love in spite of His efforts to redeem those who have turned their backs on Him.

God wanted to use the analogy to demonstrate the love and compassion He felt for the people of Israel, and us. This was something she desperately needed to overcome, the season of failure she was going through. He wanted to show her that he was all the food she needed to satisfy her hunger. Hosea bought back Gomer for fifteen shekels of silver, and one and a half homers of barley, a symbol of the value he had placed on her.

The story of Hosea is illustrative of the unending love that God has for His wayward children and how much He wants to bring us back, just like Hosea was willing to take his wife back and be a husband to her again despite her repeated acts of unfaithfulness to him. Hosea went to the extent of buying her back.

Israel would not return to the Lord their God. God wanted them to put away their false gods and love Him instead. In a similar way, Hosea pleaded with his wife, Gomer, to stay with him and end her life of prostitution so that he could be her husband.

God had great plans for Israel whom He saw as 'grapes in the wilderness, and their fathers as first fruits on the fig tree in its first season' (Hosea 9:10). Love always sees the best in a person and is willing to go beyond the faults to see the inner beauty and potential in a person. The value that is placed on us is like precious silver.

The great love chapter of 1 Corinthians 13 gives an outline of the true meaning of love in its purest form and underpins all the other gifts. These are some of the adjectives used in this chapter to describe love, which is not just an emotion but also an active expression of enduring affection.

Love is patient.

One evidence of loving someone is being patient with them. It may be at a time when they are going through a rough season in life and want to change but need some help in getting out of the condition that they are in. They may need someone to hold their hand and journey with them through some challenge that they find difficult to overcome. Maya Angelou, the inspired poet, once made a true statement that people will forget what you did, but the way you make them feel has a more lasting effect.

In any relationship, patience has a vital role to play in seeing the best in someone else. It may be in the case of someone who is experiencing any number of challenges in life. Finding ways to help them overcome through patience, love, and understanding may be very beneficial to their wellbeing.

Hosea showed patience towards his wife and gave her the gift of patience during her time of rebellion. In the same way, God is patient with us and shows love despite our choice to disobey Him. God's redeeming love always seeks to draw us back to Him.

Love is kind.

One of the best expressions of love is showing kindness to someone. Someone once said to me that even a dog will remember who feeds him and who kicks him. It is in the context of kindness that people respond in kind, and compassion shows the value we place on others.

Brotherly love is exemplified by kindness, with an unconditional love for others. The prophet Hosea was willing to remain kind to Gomer at a time when she least deserved his kindness. His compassion enabled him to reflect God's love and plan for people who were backsliding and had refused to accept God's love.

Love is not envious.

I once conducted a study of the reasons for divorce, and it was interesting to find that some couples talked about jealousy when one partner is more successful than the other. It caused a rift between them and led to arguments and misunderstanding. Whilst starting out together with love for each other, academic success or promotion for one resulted in a threatening response from the other. This led to divorce.

It would seem to be a paradox because loving someone involves wanting the best for each other. This comes through encouragement and support and a sense of contentment for blessings that cannot be measured in material terms. There is no room for pretence when there is genuine love and transparency. Love causes you to rejoice in the truth and be pleased for others when they succeed.

Love is humble.

Humility within the context of love is enormously powerful. It can involve stepping aside to allow someone else to progress, putting the needs of others above your own, and showing strength under control. Love refrains from making judgement towards others and is based on the golden rule of doing to others what you would like them to do to you.

I don't regard humility as weakness because there is strength in humility. Jesus showed humility especially when He washed the disciplines' feet. He did not consider this to be a moment of weakness but an opportunity to teach His followers the true meaning of love. Hosea was prepared to exchange his pride for humility as he repeatedly took Gomer back in the hope that she would change and reciprocate his love.

Love never fails.

True love is long-lasting and builds on a meaningful relationship. The love which Hosea had for Gomer reflected God's untiring love for the people of Israel. As I reflect this love story of Hosea and Gomer, it bears the message of redeeming love based on patience, long-suffering, and kindness.

God is forever trying to woo us back to Him because of His everlasting endurance. God wants to extend the gift of love to us as His love is steadfast and unceasing and his mercies never come to an end (Lamentations 3:22). It is an agape love that reaches out to those who do not love Him. He offers a commitment and long-suffering persistence with those who intend to go their own way.

One of my favourite songs is 'The Love of God', a classic hymn written by Frederick M. Lehman in 1917, which expressed the extensive love of God that reaches to all. It speaks of the guilty who are hemmed in with care and how the measureless love of God can forgive and how it has become a song of which the saints and angels sing.

Learning to love others and loving myself brings the greatest reflection of God's love. It is evidenced in the way I accept others with impartiality and without judgement. It involves seeing others the way Christ sees them, as people with value, and learning to respect differences. Love in its purest expression is one that puts God first then others, then us. It reaches out despite failures.

When I feel less inclined to love someone who I perceive as my enemy, I remember how God's love is unconditional, and He continues to love me due to His unfailing capacity to love. This brings a sense of satisfaction and contentment that I am accepted by Him and can benefit from the fellowship of being one of His children whom He loves, no matter what.

The chapter ends with three enduring qualities of faith, hope, and love and concluded that love is the greatest of them all.

16

OPPORTUNITY

In what ways have you seen God leading you to take advantage of an opportunity?

The gift of opportunity comes alongside a challenge to reach out and discover strengths and weaknesses about yourself. The opportunity may be shrouded in the fear of the unknown and the uncertainty that it may not be well-timed. This was not so for Zacchaeus. The timing was right for him because, as my mother often said, every disappointment is God's appointment.

There was a man named Zacchaeus who grasped the opportunity to meet Jesus. The news was travelling fast that Jesus was passing his way, and this was his opportunity to meet Him. Zacchaeus was a man whose occupation as a tax collector made him rich. Along with his wealth came a bad reputation (Luke 19).

Jesus passed through Jericho, and Zacchaeus was eager to meet him, but being a short man, he could not make his way through the crowd. His big idea was to climb up into a nearby tree, a sycamore tree, so that he would have a clear view of Jesus from a better vantage point.

When Jesus came near him, He looked up and made an invitation to Zacchaeus to come down and told him, 'Make haste and come down for today I must stay at your house' (Luke 19:5). That was an opportune moment not to be missed. Jesus may not have passed that way again, and this opportunity had now been presented to

Zacchaeus. He was able to enjoy Jesus's company in his home and made the decision there and then to be converted and change his lifestyle by repaying all those from whom he had extorted huge sums of money as a tax collector.

As an all-knowing God, He searches out those who have a sincere desire to meet Him. His divine mission is to 'save that which was lost' (Luke 19:10). He knew where Zacchaeus was. He looked up at Zacchaeus because He knew he had climbed up a tree to see Him. He meets us anywhere—in a tree, in a boat, in a crowd, or by the sea—and wants us to descend from our sycamore tree of self-reliance to have the opportunity for a personal relationship with Him.

There are limitations that need to be considered, like Zacchaeus, who was a very short man, standing in the middle of a crowd wanting to get a full view of Jesus. He took the initiative to climb up a tree. His short stature did not prevent him from finding an opportunity to meet Jesus. Opportunities come to test our willingness to step out and above the 'norm' and reach for something better.

There were those in the crowd who may have felt that Zacchaeus did not deserve the opportunity for Jesus to notice Him because of his occupation as an extortionate tax collector. Nevertheless, out of all those in the crowd, Jesus made an invitation to him to go to his house, and He dined with him. In a similar way, there may be those who are crowding our vision of Jesus to get close to Him. It requires an intentional decision to climb down from wherever we may be, to seize the opportunity to have a personal encounter with Him.

Zacchaeus grabbed the opportunity to change his former lifestyle of exploiting others in collecting taxes; he traded his way of life for spending quality time with the Master in order to become changed.

> Sometimes opportunities are not easy to spot, especially when I am busy getting on with my day-to-day activities. It may come at a time when I am not ready to jump ship from one thing to another, but it calls for a willingness to be brave like Zacchaeus, despite any limitations, and leap in when I see the time to be right.

The invitation to open the door of our hearts is an opportunity that comes alongside the promise to have fellowship with Jesus.

I recognised the gift of opportunity many years ago through poetry. It became an opening for me to share my thoughts and inspiration, and it came in a very surprising way. I was not thinking of my potential to be a poet. I was not a successful student of literature at school, but I suddenly discovered the enjoyment of writing down my thoughts in a poetic way. I did not know where it would lead; I just wanted to pen my thoughts.

It began during the early years when I attended college. There was a feeling of loneliness, being without friends amongst my other classmates, so I began to jot my thoughts down, and poetry became an emotional outlet and a new-found discovery of a gift of inspiration.

Poetry then became an incredible therapy in dealing with those unanswered questions in my life and the feeling of wanting my voice to be heard. It helped me to respond positively to the feelings I was experiencing at the time—feelings of isolation and wanting to be accepted by my peers. I felt assured that this gift could be a blessing to others, so I shared it willingly.

As the years went on, I found that the gift of penning my thoughts in general provided self-confidence. God used my season of loneliness to create a gift out of it. It became part of my worship to Him. My experience at that time gave me the opportunity to try a new skill, to overcome, examine my faith, and express my inner feelings and convictions with the need to share my story. The gift of being able to use words as a powerful tool gave me a sense of artistry, making mistakes and rewriting over and over until I reached the point where I was happy with the final product and inspiration behind the poem, having prayed over it.

I then ventured into writing articles for magazines, which sharpened my creative skill. It became my way of releasing emotions, and the inspiration began to flow. It helped to keep me focused on positive feelings, and my season of writing and receiving inspiration began. I discovered that inspiration would come at the most unusual eureka moment and became a positive way of turning valuable thoughts into a way of sharing what God has done in my life.

The key lesson I learned is not to give up on your dream or the gifts that you can inherit because they are intended for our unique blessing.

I took advantage of an opportunity in September 2014 to join a group of other poets for a poetry workshop in Alicante, Spain, for a week. I wanted to sharpen my skills and learn more about the gift of poetry. This opportunity had arrived after the publication of my second edition of inspirational poetry called *Beyond the Valley*.

The trip was intended to be a short holiday, combined with the opportunity to learn more about writing different styles of poetry from some renowned experts and sharing with a group of like-minded poets who had a similar interest. It was a great opportunity to examine other people's work and share thoughts from what they had written. I became more appreciative of positive criticism, and their critique was very helpful in shaping my views of how different we all view the world and our situations in a very creative way.

As an added blessing, I met a couple and became good friends. They lived not far away from my hometown, and we kept in contact afterwards. The opportunity then came when they invited me to be one of their guests at a poetry evening event to share my book of poems with their regular attendees in the community of Hertfordshire.

Opportunity may present itself as a gift and is in the making during the most unexpected times, especially when a door is closed to you and another one opens in quick succession. This gift of opportunity is there to take an instinctive response to the challenge, which may come only once or sometimes many times over in a different form if the advantage to take hold of chances did not happen the first time.

There are poetry writing courses which provide the right techniques and styles of writing, and these are all useful for personal development. Poetry evenings provide opportunities to improve your skill.

Saying yes to an opportunity may involve developing a keen eye for areas that may be of interest and seeking out people who are able and willing to support and help along the way to achieve a particular objective.

As doors are opened, the time may be right for spotting your gift and preparing you for a new venture that realises your dream and takes you to a challenging time of discovery. Whatever the opportunity is, there is always something new in store for us. Life never stops changing, and the seasons that we go through can be a journey of self-development and enhancement.

17

SUCCESS

Success is failure turned inside out, the silver tint on the clouds
of doubt, and you never can tell how close you ae, it may be near
when it seems so far. So stick to the fight when you're hardest
hit, it's when things seem worse that you must not quit.
(Unknown)

How do you measure success? What lessons can you share about
failure and success?

The inspirational poem called *'The Race'* by D. H. Groberg tells
the story of a boy who lined up to run in a children's race. He was
full of hope that he could come first or even hoped for a tie. There
was excitement as the whistle blew, and these young runners started
off. One of the boys' dads was watching eagerly and cheering his son
on, but the boy encountered a shallow dip and fell. He got up and
continued to run, and his mind was focused on how proud his dad
would be if he won.

He could hear the cheering of the crowd, and again he slipped
and fell as his arms were all over the place. Each time he fell, he got
up and continued to run the race, despite the feeling of defeat until
he reached the finishing line.

There were tears as defeat was beating down on him, but the
encouraging words were to get up and start again. The gift of success

came in the reality of perseverance to make it to the finish line, because we are stronger when we fail and get up than when we never try at all. That was the message of achievement, that life is just like that, with its 'twists and turns', and all that is needed is to get up and start again (Bennett).

An outstanding example of success motivated by contentment for God's plan is seen in the life of Joseph in Genesis 37. He was a young man aged seventeen years old who had a dream of becoming a successful leader in the home. He had been loved by his father, who gave him the gift of a coat of many colours, much to the jealousy of his brothers who hated him for it and whose sole intent was to kill and get rid of him.

He shared the details of his dream his dreams with his father and brothers. The first dream occurred in a scene where they were 'binding sheaves in the field and Joseph's sheaf stood upright and the brothers' sheaves bowed down to his sheaf' (Genesis 37:7). This was followed by another dream in which Joseph saw 'the sun, the moon and eleven stars' all bowing down to him (Genesis 37:9).

All this became too much for Joseph's brothers who concluded that Joseph's implication to his dreams was one of dominion over them. This led to his brothers being filled with such hatred and jealousy that they seized an opportunity to throw him into a pit and then sold him to some Ishmaelites for twenty shekels of silver.

The dream seemingly ended with his destination in Egypt, being sold into slavery in the house of Potiphar and his wife. Potiphar's wife tried unsuccessfully to seduce him during this time, which was a bad thing, but he was able to get away from her and resisted the temptation to sin against God, which was a good outcome. This led to him being falsely accused and thrown into prison. The dream of success was even more remote at this time, but God was with Joseph.

Joseph was now in close quarters in the prison with a butler and a baker. His wisdom of being able to interpret their dreams resulted in his release from prison, as he was also able to interpret the dream of Pharaoh, king of Egypt. The dream lived on when Joseph's accurate interpretation brought him recognition and success from Pharoah.

Success begins with a dream and a vision. It is sometimes accompanied by setbacks, disappointments, and roadblocks along the way. When God steps in, our dreams become a reality.

Joseph's dream of success finally came when he was promoted to a position of leadership as prime minister in Egypt, second only in command to the king. He forgave his brothers and said to them, 'As for you, you meant evil against me, but God meant it for good, in order to bring it about as it is this day, to save many people alive' (Genesis 50:20).

I recently received an email from a friend, which I thought was extremely encouraging and helpful to me, and I would like to share it. It's called the 'Seven Sisters of Success' (author unknown). The email gave an account of several groups of extremely successful people who were interviewed. There were artists, politicians, athletes, writers, and multimillionaires who were interviewed. When asked for the key or essential factors that allowed them to accomplish so much, they gave these answers:

1. Self-awareness. It was the idea of understanding who they were with values and goals that were important to them. Of course, there were regrets and setbacks, but they used them as steppingstones and not roadblocks.
2. They were eager, confident, and optimistic about the future.
3. They all had written thirty-day goals and performance targets that could be achievable.
4. They realised the importance of family and friends and networked well, having mentors who coached them in various skills, which provided valuable lessons for them.
5. Honesty and good time management were important, and they remained approachable and used precision to identify the important things in life.

What had impressed the interviewer above all else was the fact that their successes were not related to family or background. They had not been born wealthy, and only about half completed college. They did not seem destined for success. They did not make their fortunes in high tech or winning large sums of money. Instead, they followed a plan that created persistent high levels of success.

These extremely successful people knew what they wanted, and through hard work and perseverance, they were able to gain success.

When one door is closed, God opens many more, a step at a time. Success can come when prayer is all it takes to make a difference because God always has something better when we face failure, because He is a God of opportunity.

I once discovered an interesting story of a famous painter named James Whistler. He was born in 1834. He lived in the United States and was educated in France. His goal of becoming an army general failed miserably. He was driven by this goal above everything else, but it never materialised.

His life was revolutionised when he discovered that he could paint, and through a paradigm shift in his thinking, his failure was turned into success and later became a famous painter known for his famous painting called *Whistler's Mother*. From then on, Whistler produced many oil paintings of artistic value. His invention came as a result of failure.

Success is usually recognised in those who are willing to go the extra mile, above and beyond expectation. It can defy the most incredible circumstances that hinder success. It shows up when you refuse to give up or give in to failure.

I have learned that human effort cannot be compared with God's divine purpose. I interpret the experience as a test that may be leading me to something with far greater benefits. Instead, I continue to trust in the God of possibilities and impossibilities.

The Father's will brings success out of failure and a future with Him that will last. As He wipes away all traces of mistakes, I can be confident that within the secret shades of my life, He is there to carry me through to the finishing line.

Look out for success when you have tried and given your best. All your efforts have been spent and overspent to those things you desired the most. Only in retrospect, the blessings are counted. At those times, you had refused to give up, giving time and energies without the end in sight.

You know in your heart that there had to be a purpose! And pushing against a tide of struggling emotions, you feel the odds do not add up, it seems. Then you see dreams becoming a reality. Tears are washed away by laughter of friends; family ties become stronger. The waiting had to be worth it, and lifetime experiences produce growth.

> Success can come at a time when prayer is what it takes to make a difference. When the things you long for begin to emerge, success is now ready to take hold of you.

Success that came on the heels of failure happened on 20 January 2021, when the world historically witnessed the inauguration of President Joe Biden and Vice President Kamala Harris. It was reported that this was the president's third attempt to take up this office, having served as vice president in the past. Like Joseph, his goal had never left him. Through persistence, he finally became the president of the United States of America as he won the election with resounding success.

While on a recent visit to one of my favourite seaside resorts, I travelled on a guided bus tour around the beautiful city of Brighton and Hove in Sussex, England. As I listened to the interesting and historical commentary on these towns, I learned that Winston Churchill first began his educational journey here. However, he did not get on very well because of his unsettling behaviour. His early days of education did not turn out right, yet his failure still became an outstanding example of times when failure is not the determinant defining moment in life. It is built around the success of those who want to transform it into the silver tint on the clouds of doubt.

Churchill said, 'Success is not final; failure is not final: it is the courage to continue that counts.' Success is therefore ongoing, and so failure is not the end. It is the courage to continue that becomes a measurement of success. Nothing in life is ever final because there are higher things we can achieve when we do not rely on past achievements or rest on our laurels. Failure can be used as a learning tool. Get up each time you fall. It takes courage to do that, so congratulate yourself for the courage to begin again.

When life is broken for whatever reason and in the middle of the darkest season, you can still submit the brokenness to God as you journey through life. It's like a child whose crayon is broken but finds that he/she can still draw a beautiful picture.

God is all powerful at putting broken pieces together and producing success despite failure. As we acknowledge and appreciate His help, He will enable you to produce an outstanding piece of work on your life's canvass that others can be blessed by and gain inspiration from.

18

PARENTING

Behold children are a heritage of the Lord.
The fruit of the womb is a reward.
Psalm 127:3

Have you been given the gift of parenting, and how has it shaped your life as a great role model?

My gift of parenting was one of the most challenging yet rewarding gifts I have ever been given by the Lord. This season in my life began a transformational process that took time to unwrap. At the same time, it is indeed a blessing and a gift from the Lord with the opportunity to train and influence the development of my family to become leaders in their own right.

I followed my mother's example of inviting me by her bedside for morning prayers to start the day. I continued this legacy, which became an important part of their growing up together as we prayed about all the issues that confronted them as youngsters. We placed problems before the Lord to request the gift of His blessing and protection throughout the fluctuating seasons of their own lives.

The gift of parenting involved the ability to become a role model and leader in the home. It involved learning about yourself as well as your children and is a special gift for those who enjoy the pleasure of raising little people to become responsible adults. It demands time, patience, sacrifice, support, and hard work, all underpinned by love to train and allow a child to understand the importance of discipline, obedience, boundaries, and a space to be themselves.

The gift of parenting does not come with a blueprint as many parents will agree, but what it has given me is the opportunity to learn while leading and accepting the challenge to become an example.

The role that prayer plays has been always an anchor, and times of rejoicing came with answered prayers. Reliance on God to get me through a season of uncertainty gave me the strength and courage to forge ahead, knowing that it is worth the struggle.

When thinking about the gift of parenting, I often use the analogy of building a bridge. You never know how strong the bridge is until traffic comes along and good workmanship is tested, and you get that sense of relief that you didn't do that bad after all!

The test of effective parenting is seen in the growth of a child. As the preparation is done in early life, you patiently wait as over time the strength of the 'bridge' you built is tested depending on the kind of foundation that is laid at the beginning. The carrying capacity of the bridge (foundation) is then proven as they set out in life on their own, and the full weight of your training supports them.

I once shared the above analogy with a consultant psychiatrist I worked with. His daughter had gone to university and graduated with flying colours. He came to work full of excitement and feeling elated and proud that his daughter had reached her goal. He also felt that the hardship and sacrifice of getting her to that goal was worth it. He was impressed with my analogy and thanked me for sharing the truth of that statement with him.

Parenting taught me many valuable lessons, like how to be patient as growth is not an overnight experience. The long process of living and learning is a season of adaptation and responding to your children and the investment of their happiness. Being a good role model to my children was important in avoiding the saying 'Do what I say, not what I do'. It is a God-given responsibility for making decisions and accepting that mistakes are inevitable but are learning platforms.

I find that having a spirit of contentment and peace, even when things are not going your way, helps to stay calm and connected to God's plan as He is a caring Father. I am humbled by the fact that God can reward us with beautiful gifts when we are totally reliant on Him and place our children in His hands to do what we cannot do on our own. I am pleased to say that my two children are now very successful and responsible adults who are exemplary leaders in their field of careers. They are now replicating the gift and passing it on to their own children.

Jesus was a great role model who often spoke to His followers in parables so that they could identify and relate to His teachings. The parables were a simple illustration that had a moral and spiritual truth.

There is a parable recorded in Luke 15:11–32 of a family that comprised a father and two sons. The younger of the two sons wanted his own independence, far away from the love and parenting of his father. The son who is known as the prodigal son began to cause division in the home by his choice to leave his father's home and launch out on his own.

He was no longer contented with living under his father's roof, and filled with a sense of entitlement, he said to his father, 'Give me the portion of goods that falls to me' (Luke 15:12). His father complied with his request and divided the inheritance between the two sons, giving him his portion to use in whatever way he wished.

The prodigal son went into a 'far country', which implied that he wanted to distance himself as far away as possible from his father to the bright lights and carefree living. The money was wasted amongst friends until it was all gone, and he had no money and no friends. He learned the hard way that sometimes these two go together.

The young man's quest for independence provided the opportunity to indulge in a lifestyle that was contrary to the values upheld in his father's home. His selfish motive of wanting his inheritance prematurely showed his failure to appreciate the security of his father's love and provision that was always available to him. He underestimated the freedom he had enjoyed over the years.

Misfortune suddenly came when an unexpected famine arrived, and by this time, all his money was gone. He had to find another way of survival. By now, he was destitute and a long way from home. He was prepared to take on any job that was offered to him, which happened to be a job feeding pigs. It was at this pivotal point in his life that he realised how far he had come from home and his father's love and provision for him as a son and not a hired servant.

He made his way back home, armed with a speech of repentance, and pleaded his father's forgiveness to take him back. He was even prepared to work for him as one of the servants. He forgot that no matter how far away he had been, he was still his father's son, no matter how unworthy he may have felt.

There are many things that inspired me about this parable of the prodigal son. The focus is not solely on what the son had done but on his father's response to his waywardness. It illustrates the love of God who is willing and ready to welcome back home all those who have gone away from His love.

It was not his father's intention to disown him for his unwise decision. Instead of judging his son, he gave him wings while at the same time had longed for the day when he would return home or at least change his attitude of entitlement. When the father saw his son making his way back home again, he ran to meet him and 'fell on his neck and kissed him' (Luke 15:20).

The gracious disposition of his father welcomed his son back, even though he smelt like what he had been through. The father was not interested in his lovely speech that he had prepared on his way back home, he just wanted his son to say the words 'Daddy I'm home again". This is what mattered most to his father, and he forgave him. A celebration party was then prepared for him as he was welcomed back. The son was reinstated with the best robe and a ring, along with the finest food he could have to satisfy his hunger (Luke 15:22–24).

After he had squandered all his inheritance he was now ready to take on a servant's role in his father's house, if only he could be welcomed back home. This story showcases the loving forgiveness and benevolence of a parent with a gracious disposition. These are all the qualities of the gift of parenting.

The parable also exemplifies the love that God has for those who run away from Him and the measure of forgiveness He offers. It is in this recognition that we discover that the Father is waiting and longing to receive us back and to reinstate the relationship we once had with Him. It is a great lesson of someone who recognises how much he/she is valued even though they have gone astray.

The prodigal son had the opportunity to be accountable for his actions and sought forgiveness and restitution from his father. This is an important aspect of parenting when children are taught to be accountable for their actions and recognition of consequences that follow from bad choices. He eventually realised how he had wasted his father's wealth and disregarded his love. Being led by his conscience, he did the right thing in pleading his father's forgiveness and reinstatement back into the family.

From this story, I consider the father in the prodigal son's story to be the hero who was waiting expectantly and watching patiently for his son's return. He never gave up on the day when he could reinstate his son. He allowed him the freedom yet at the same time longed for their relationship to be restored.

The father's bridge was tested when he agreed to let his son go and experience life for himself. He gave him wings to experience life on his own, in the hope that he would be responsible in making good choices. Like the prodigal's father, the gift of parenting involves the opportunity to be loving and give children freedom while at the same time providing love and security when things go wrong. It should never be the case of 'I told you so'.

Being a member of God's family is a special privilege, which is eternal, and showcases God as a tender, loving Father who parents His children and never gives up on them even when they fall through the cracks. He then lovingly picks them up.

He knows His children and permits personal choices. He entrusts the gift of parenting to be used as good stewards. It is wonderful how God can use dreadful seasons to teach dependence on Him and for His glory. It becomes the masterful work of the potter and his clay. His shaping has been gradual, sometimes painful, but always beautiful on reflection.

Janet Brown has written an insightful blog on four parenting styles:

1. Authoritative
2. Authoritarian

3. Permissive
4. Neglectful

These styles indicate the way a child will grow and develop and how the parents' influence can bring either a successful or a disastrous outcome. Janet Brown said that the authoritative parent is firm but fair, and this has the effect of nurturing a successful child. The authoritarian parent is demanding and is usually accompanied by punishment for disobedience. The child being raised with this kind of parent learns how to be resentful towards the parent. A permissive parent fails to enforce rules and boundaries. Lastly, the child that experiences neglectful parenting, becomes a risk to himself/herself, and this leads to an unhealthy life (Brown).

Being raised by my mother after the death of my father provided an opportunity of experiencing how my mother handled discipline in an authoritative way and how everything was part of teaching me how to handle challenges that I would face on my own. She prepared me for life by her example which was fair yet firm. It was the bridge that I was able to walk on. Her love and sharing have helped me to admire and develop these qualities as I became an adult.

Unwrapping the gift of parenting has meant the responsibility and accountability for providing sound principles and to harness their inherent abilities and capabilities as they grew up in the world. As young parents now, it is a time for them to put into practice what they were taught and to teach it in turn to their own children. The gift of contentment was always the guide in teaching the crucial lesson of avoiding comparison with others and being happy with who they are. I often instilled values in my children, one of which was 'you are not better than anyone else, but you are just as good as everyone else.'

The affirmation that is given to a child has long-lasting consequences, and although I experienced some tough seasons along the way, it became character-building. It is good when a parent teaches a child adaptability, understanding, and self-awareness and that human frailty is a part of growing up to appreciate that his/her parent is not perfect. It produces a strong parent-child bond that leads to trust, confidence, and connection with the outside world.

Giving children the opportunity to know God as their Father and Friend and involving them in family worship builds their trust in

God, knowing that prayer is an important element in their journey. It prepares them, I believe, for the seasons that will inevitably come and carries them along the bridge of life. It supports them with the knowledge of who they can turn to in a crisis, or when reaching a crossroads, they find direction in making the right choices.

Over the years, I have learned many lessons about being a role model. My children survived the hardships, the scratches on their knees, falling off bikes, and getting up again My role was to encourage them during these times not to give up on their ideals in life. Facing problems and disappointments was a challenge as I had to draw on my own inner resources of coping to pass it on to them. There were times of hardship when I couldn't afford the latest fashion to keep up with their friends, but it was also a time of letting them see the value of delayed gratification.

The season of parenting means talking through problems and not taking each other too seriously or for granted. There is wisdom in letting your child know that you love them, believe in them, and will support them in whatever choices they make, especially when they are considered to be wise choices.

My late mother had a great and lasting influence on me, and I learned a lot about parenting from her example. I felt closer to her as she parented me within a dual role. As the years went on, I considered her as my friend as she would say, 'I'm not just your mother, but I am also your friend'—a relationship which she fostered by being a confidant and an approachable mother.

I knew I could talk to my mother about anything that concerned me, and we spent many precious hours talking and laughing together. She had a great sense of humour that would sometimes defuse situations. She had panache and style and possessed a smile that would charm the birds from the tree, so to speak.

She was blessed with a caring and sympathetic attitude, with good listening skills. Whenever my season changed and there was a problem to be solved, she was always there to provide her support. She instilled the belief that prayer would provide a better prospect of keeping us together. The phrase 'let's have a word of prayer' was never far from her lips. It became a strong family ethic, a principle that I have been able to emulate in my own family as a much-needed influence today.

I often reflected on my mother's ability to problem-solve. I recognised that she had a focused attitude and accepted the gifts that God had given her. Indeed, it was after my father's death that she took the initiative to find work in England and paved the way for my reunion with her after one year of necessary separation in Barbados. She tempered the gift of parenting with love, warmth, and wisdom. There were boundaries which I knew had to be recognised, and my mother had a way of commanding my respect but never demanded it.

Experiencing a life of contentment highlights challenges and learning curves. The gift of parenting is no exception. Walking in the example of the way we are parented as God's children gives a pattern that is the ultimate blueprint.

19

PEACE

These things I have spoken to you, that in Me you may
have peace; in the world you will have tribulation but
be of good cheer, I have overcome the world
John 16:33

What are some practical steps that you can take to have peace
for whatever you face in life?

Without peace in our lives, the scene can look like the weather
conditions of the year 2020 in the United Kingdom, which began with
three storms and was the wettest on record. The storm called Ceira
devastated many homes with flooding and strong winds in places like
Scotland and Wales. Then came storm Denis a few weeks later, with
strong winds, more flooding and loss of homes. The Army was called
in and sandbags placed by the doors of houses to stop the surging of
flooding that swept across Devon and Cornwall. There was a yellow
alert where some roads turned into rivers.

The desire to maintain a peaceful disposition is a gift for your
seasons with all the disturbances, confusion, and uncertainty all
around us on a local and global level. There are many things that
can make an impact on our peace such as rising prices, the quest for
climate change, conflicting news and what the future holds.

Peace reaches deep within us, and gives a reason to be happy
and joyful, experiencing a sense of quietness in the middle of stormy

weather. Despite everything that is going on, peace can be described as a bird perched on the tree, resting its whole self on the branch, and experiencing total peace from what is going on beneath it.

Peace is an extremely rare commodity in today's world. Without Christ at the helm of our endeavours the seasons of life can be as devastating as storms Ceira or Denis. Paul, the writer of Romans, knew this quite well and admonished the people of Rome to make a concerted effort to follow peace. In this way, we can better build one another up. Peace always diffuses hate and strife, and when we aim to make peace our goal rather than cause friction and anger, we live in harmony not only with others but also with ourselves.

We are more inclined to bring forgiveness and understanding into a situation when we are in an attitude of peace and tranquillity. Peace is not the absence of problems, but problems are less likely to overwhelm us.

Peace is a gift and a choice. I can choose to unwrap the gift of peace as it is my best arsenal in the battle against the constant bombardment of tragedies and daily news. I can choose to be constantly aware of the influence of the Holy Spirit to impart a state of inner peace. I remain sensitive yet not oblivious to what is going on. By taking this free offer of peace, it enables me to remain unperturbed in the knowledge that God is in control.

During lockdown to control the spread of the Corona Virus, I decided to take up some hobbies, so I began writing this book. The notes and thoughts had begun some time ago, but now was a good time to focus my attention to things that would increase my sense of inner harmony and wellbeing. It became a great distraction aimed at feeling less stressed about what was happening at the time. Admittedly, there were times when I felt overwhelmed by the number of deaths that were recorded daily but remaining in a season of prayer about these sad times helped me to respond to the news in a peaceful and prayerful way.

I know that all good gifts come from God, so the gift of peace is good and lasting. It does not have an expiry date or become out of fashion like an iPad that needs upgrading from time to time. This is a gift for a lifetime with amazing results and a guarantee that it will help me to overcome whatever I may face in life.

The gift of inner peace will be a precious one to me that will help me to relax and receive assurance that God is always with me. The gift is unique and custom-made for those who wish to accept it and enjoy every season regardless of external circumstances. No one else can give it or take it away because it becomes part of your inner self, personality, and uniqueness. It is gift-wrapped with the covering of God's love and protection over your life.

It is not a gift that can be replicated by anyone else in the world. His peace allows you to remain 'untroubled' by happenings yet remaining focused and secure in the knowledge that God is in control. Therefore, it does not leave you feeling oblivious to life and situations, but it helps you to deal with challenges in a different way, without allowing yourself to become perturbed. It's reassuring to know that Jesus is in the boat so that we can smile at the storm, as my mother often reminded me.

A peaceful and calm spirit has a contagious effect that brings hope and serenity to others who are troubled and find it difficult to be at peace with their struggle. It can be sensed by those around us even when we are not aware of the calm spirit that we are carrying.

This reminds me of a meeting I attended once a few years ago, when a case was being discussed about a client who was suffering with deep depression and feeling hopeless about her life and her reason for living. There were professionals attending the meeting along with some of the patient's family members. At the end of the meeting, I left the room to return home. As I made my way out of the building where the meeting took place, I met one of the managers who told me that the patient told her, "whatever that lady has, I want some of it". I was impressed but gave God the glory as He is the one who allows peace to shine around us when we are unaware of His presence. I will treasure this gift as one that I can use every day to cope with the stresses in my own life while becoming a witness to those who are desperately seeking peace to calm their troubled spirits.

The word *peace* is often understood as a time when there is freedom from war or work or worry. It may even be recognised as a time of financial freedom, having job satisfaction, and enjoying an excellent standard of living. The absence of worry can also be deemed as a time of peace and harmony and associated with a period of quietness, with no noise around you or fear of anything that would threaten the sense of calmness and serenity.

I believe that God's gift of peace cannot be defined as the absence of strife, but peace can be experienced in the midst of it. It is a calm response to challenges, and the best example of this is a prayer that was written by a US theologian in the 1940–50s. In this prayer, he asked God for serenity to be able to distinguish between the things that can be changed and those that cannot be changed and to gain wisdom in knowing the difference. The difference is what makes all the difference.

The *Desiderata* has been very meaningful to me because it relates to peace as the essence of life where peace with God and us can make a difference. Having a sense of 'Live and let live' exchanges the bad experiences for the good and seeks harmony that defies confusion and strife.

I regard peace as a way of overcoming evil with good responses and brokenness with wholesomeness through a peaceable attitude. Therefore, peace is not being in a state of calm where everything is in perfect order. On the contrary, it helps to maintain a sense of tranquillity which overrides each troubling season. The gift of God's peace recognises that the world indeed is a beautiful place to live in. Inward peace cannot be taken away or influenced by what is going on around you.

When Jesus was leaving His disciples after the rResurrection, He bequeathed a special gift to them. He left the legacy of His peace, which was not dependent on good times. He knew that tough times were ahead for them and the gift of peace would help them to cope with persecution and suffering for the cause of Christ (John 14:27).

There are many references to peace in the Bible, and one of my favourites records is the time when Jesus stilled the storm, which is recorded in two gospels, Matthew 8 and Mark 4. The miracle of Jesus stilling the storm happened after Jesus had been preaching to the crowds.

On this occasion, Jesus went with the disciples in a boat, and not long afterwards, a great storm came. Jesus was asleep, and the disciples became afraid and woke Him up when the water was filling the boat. He immediately spoke to the wind and waves, saying, 'Peace be still.' Immediately after hearing the voice of Jesus, the seas and waves obeyed the voice of their Maker, bringing stillness and calmness to the waters (Mark 4:39).

As I reflected on the power of Jesus to still the storm, the winds and waves recognised the voice of Him who called creation into being from the beginning. He spoke the words of peace and it was so. He is the very quintessence of peace and still speaks the Word into our storms today and works things out to our ultimate good. He knows exactly how to handle life's seasons because He is the stiller of the storm. Jesus promised the kind of special peace that would go beyond all possible understanding (Philippians 4:7) that runs like the Mississippi River in North Minnesota, USA.

The year 2020 will always be remembered as a year in history when a global pandemic caused by the coronavirus resulted in millions of deaths around the world. It affected the economy, businesses, travel, worship, education, and social life as we know it. It became a huge wake-up call that life cannot be taken for granted, and the things that were thought to be things we could not live without were the things we had to live without, like social distancing, showing affection like hugging, holding hands, and keeping each one safe from the virus.

During this time, there was a tremendous increase in mental health illnesses. The medical profession was overworked with insufficient beds. The need for peace became a priority as the safety and preservation of lives were at risk. Sadness and daily loss of loved ones threatened the hope and peace of many who sought meaning to personal and worldwide tragedy and untimely separation from loved ones. Yet even at a time like a global pandemic, there were answered prayers, and God's gift of inner peace could be achieved. It impacted the lives of all who prayed for peace and a stilling of the storm that raged all around us.

At this and all other times, I began to pray for my heart to be still. Yet, from a human point of view, I remember the times when I literally broke down in tears, praying for God to intervene and help the nation and save the world from the dreaded invisible enemy. I needed to be at peace and centre my thoughts on the eternal God who can control everything, even the storms, and not allow my heart to be filled with despair. In the end, taking one day at a time was the only solution for me and finding ways to occupy my thoughts.

I used the weapon of prayer to focus on God's power to bring healing to our world. God was true to His Word and remained faithful. It began to keep my mind and heart centred in Christ Jesus as the great controller of any storm. In this season of life, it is important to find serenity despite turmoil and to receive the wisdom to distinguish between what we can change and what we cannot change. This helps us to enjoy whatever season we are in.

The provision of technology, like Zoom and WhatsApp, meant that although church attendance was suspended, there was still an opportunity to have virtual worship and remain connected with the believers. This has been a tremendous blessing to feel a sense of peace at a time of restrictions.

One of my role models is Mandela, who became the first black president of South Africa. His autobiography is called *Mandela: The Authorized Portrait* and is a study of the history of this phenomenal leader. I became inspired by his unwavering quest for peace despite his imprisonment and unjust treatment which he suffered for twenty-seven years. He has been revered around the world as a pioneer for peace in the face of injustice and brought freedom to many.

He was recognised as one who had embraced the gift of peace even when everything around him was demanding a different response to undeserved suffering during the time of apartheid in South Africa. Through Mandela's peace initiative, he was able to bring an end of apartheid through peaceful protests, eventually gaining the Nobel Peace Prize in 1993. He won the hearts of everyone who respected him as someone who refused to allow hatred and unforgiveness to get in the way of progress for his people.

When Mandela died in 2013, he left a legacy to the world that helps people to understand that peace is a characteristic that God wants us to adopt against the backdrop of strife and disagreements. Mandela experienced peace and, ultimately, freedom that was outside the confines of his cell. His example showed that freedom can also be experienced when we allow our minds to be transported from a difficult season to where we would like things to be.

Paul, the writer of the book of Romans, accepted the gift of peace, and in his address to the Colossians, he said, 'Let the peace of God rule in your hearts' (Colossians 3:15). In this way, building one another up becomes possible in the pursuit of peace and happiness.

There is so much today that could disturb our peace—rising prices, debt, separation, breakdown of relationships, illness, political unrest, and so on. Peace is not surrendering our rights, but it maintains our values of becoming strong and determined about what we know to be right.

Being right with God brings peace. His assurance in my heart eliminates the need to worry but choosing to trust in God. Through prayer, I can become a peace-loving person by allowing Him to work things out as He makes me part of that working-out process. Therefore 'in quietness and confidence shall be your strength' (Isaiah 30:15).

God's peace is perfectly flawless and endures forever. It is a special kind of peace that has been gifted to believers who love to obey God's law, and it brings a great sense of serenity to those who comply with His will.

God's peace reaches into the heart where reliance on Him makes the difference to my reactions to life's upsetting plans and allows the divine purpose to override fear or anxiety. I acknowledge that goodness and truth will triumph in the end.

The gift of peace is transformational, with an inner stillness that transcends the things that are happening, like a pandemic. This gift challenges the way we respond to the various changes in life.

The weapon of prayer is the only effective defence in maintaining fortitude as the journey through the seasons of chaos and disappointment threaten a sense of peace. Amongst my survival kit, the quiet place, either in my mind or around me, helps to exclude those annoying things that tend to unravel you at the wrong time. At these times, I have experienced the joy and contentment of talking to people you can trust, as sharing our concerns provides a therapeutic outlet.

20

PRAISE

Rejoice in the Lord, O you righteous, for
praise from the upright is beautiful.
Psalm 33:1

Do you find it difficult to praise God when going through a
time of suffering?

The theme of praise links in well with the attitude of gratitude
that brings renewal, whatever the season we may be in. It defies the
difficult situation you are in and lifts you out of despair. It becomes
an outward expression of thanksgiving that comes from a heartfelt
appreciation for what God has done. Praise is something that brings
pleasure to God because He is always at the centre of a praise that
brings glory to Him, being worthy of our praise.

During the apostle Paul's successful missionary journey, he came
to Derby and Lystra (Acts 16). It was there that he met a very well-
spoken disciple named Timothy, whose father was Greek and his
mother was Jewish. Paul wanted Timothy to accompany him but,
before doing so, had to satisfy the Jewish tradition of circumcision,
knowing that Timothy had a Jewish background.

The journey took them through areas like Troas, Neapolis, and
Macedonia, where they stayed for a few days. On the Sabbath day,
they went out of the city for prayer, according to custom, and spoke

to some women there. They were both met with a challenge as a slave girl who was possessed by evil spirits began to follow them, which went on for a few days.

Paul and Silas were thrown into prison for their faith by healing the girl from the demonic spirit which had possessed her. She had been taunting them about the fact that they were recognised as men of the true God. Annoyed by her constant mocking, Paul spoke out and rebuked the evil spirit in her, which had immediate results as the evil spirit left her.

This sparked a negative response from the crowd who had, up until now, been profiting from her fortune-telling occupation. The people's main concern stemmed from their exploitation of her rather than her mental welfare and the fact that she was under the influence of an evil spirit.

Paul and Silas were both taken before the magistrates. They were now subjected to public humiliation in the marketplace. Their clothes were torn off, and they were beaten and thrown into a cell (Acts 16:23).

In the deep cell, they began to lift their voices in worship and singing hymns. It became a witness to the other prisoners who were listening. There is no better time to praise God than at the midnight of your life when you are hemmed in by circumstances and can't find a way out. It can happen when you are standing up for the Gospel as Paul and Silas were.

The miracle of release came at midnight when their chains became loosened after an earthquake, and the prison guard, who was asleep at the time, woke up scared and was about to kill himself, thinking that they had escaped. Paul then shouted out to reassure the guard that they had not escaped. A conversion then took place as the guard, astounded by what had happened, trembled and cried out to be saved, and he and his household were saved that day.

The chains fell off when they witnessed the power of deliverance through faith and praising God in hard seasons. "God responded in an amazing way. He shook the foundations of the prison so violently that all its doors opened wide, and the chains felt off the prisoner's feet and wrists" (Macarthur).

Paul and Silas's experience is inspirational as it teaches that despite the path we travel, praise can be a solution that brings release and coping strategies. As anxiety is so prevalent in our society today, it affects our mental and physical health, so praise can bring a sense of serenity and contentment. This may not mean that the problem will be immediately resolved, but praise seems to have a calming effect while in a state of worship.

Praising and singing has been one of the greatest therapeutic tools I can use against the temptation to be downhearted. It provides strength to focus on my ideal in life. Against all odds, singing brings hope for better things to come as I hold on despite every test. It becomes my song of faith that reaches beyond what I cannot see to what I can believe.

Giving praise to God during Paul's difficult situation was a huge witness despite being incarcerated for their belief. Paul and Silas were motivated to sing and give praise and thanks to God, even at a time when their faith was tested.

My reason for singing originates from a place where, despite the season, I can still raise my song of faith that reinforces my convictions. I do not have to wait for thigs to turn out right before I can praise Him. The gift of praise dispels discouraging moments as I refuse to give in to external pressure. A song of faith enables strength to hold on to the best despite every test. I have found that at these times, singing breaks through the clouds of doubt.

I reinforce the memory that God has stepped in for me at numerous times and answered prayers. Having no answers to prayer is also a reason to sing my way out of it regardless and praise Him through worshipful singing that keeps me in connection with God and His will, not mine.

Singing has many health benefits. It reduces stress and improves self-confidence. The voice box is such an intricate instrument gifted to us by our Creator. The larynx, as its commonly known, is created from cartilage which comprises small bands of tissue. These bands expand, with connections that adjust the sounds from the air we breathe. This strengthens the view that everyone can sing if there is a willingness to practise, tone, train, and develop the voice to sing.

One of my favourite all-time singers is Andrea Bocelli, the Italian tenor. Even though he became blind at the age of twelve after a soccer match, Bocelli developed his gift of music, spanning both classical and pop genres. His rendering of the 'Lord's Prayer' is moving as he draws the hearers into this beautiful song with his gift of singing.

Andrea Bocelli's love of music and his gift of singing was encouraged by his mother, and he was taught to play many instruments, including the flute, piano, and saxophone. This encourages me to know that even in our disabilities, God can shower free gifts for the journey.

There are so many favourite hymns that I love to sing because the lyrics are comforting, and I resonate with them as a part of worship, giving glory and praise to God. Singing can be used to elevate the mood, producing happiness and joy. Expressing ourselves through singing can be delightful to hear. If sung well, it can be emotionally uplifting.

Singing in a choir provides a disciplined way of singing by listening to each other's voices and developing self-confidence in using the gift as a group. It can be a great social and communication tool. I once visited an old people's home with a choir and sang Christmas carols. They really enjoyed the visit, and singing carols created a festive atmosphere. We watched their faces light up as we sang to them. People respond to the melody of singing, especially gospel music, that soothes spirits and cheers them up.

I remember some years ago while working with some team members at a local hospital, and they joined a choir to sing to the patients called Singing for the Terrified. When I heard the name, I assumed they were referring to the patients, but the 'terrified' was them! They would often claim that they didn't have a singing voice and wanted to gain the confidence to overcome the fear of singing in front of others. It can have a soothing effect to mentally ill patients and those who are feeling isolated and lonely. It is used to improve mental stress and the immune system and even helps us to have a good night's sleep, like the soothing sounds of David on his harp playing beautifully to King Saul to relieve his troubled spirit.

Over the years, the experiences of singing and listening to beautiful music brought me out of situations. It lifted my spirit, increased my faith and hope, and created an avenue for releasing praise to God. It is reassuring to know that singing can bring me closer to my Heavenly Father. This is a source of certainty.

The psalmist David re-echoed his praise throughout the Psalms to glorify God as a form of worship and acknowledgement of His goodness and ability to keep His promises and to sustain him despite failures. He believed in a God who transforms and renews the humble soul who comes in recognition of His greatness. He expressed God's kindness, graciousness, and loving character, so praise becomes beautiful.

The gift of singing tunes my heart at the time when I think I have least to rejoice about, but at those times of praise through singing and thanksgiving, it reinforces my need to recognise the measure of blessing that I receive.

Paul and Silas found this to be true as the chains fell, and God was given the praise for protecting them at a time of persecution for their faith.

God is worthy of praise at any time, and He expects me to come into His presence with singing and worshipping Him. It lifts my spirit and has a rejuvenating way of transporting my thoughts to see things clearer. Praise through the gift of singing raises my expectations in what God can do in the future.

For the past few years, my family and I have shared prayer sessions together as a small ministry group of intercession for others. The prayer group comprises six sisters, two brothers-in-law, and a newly joined Christian friend. The practice of praying together has been a lifelong legacy left by my mother, who instilled in us the importance of family worship, with the thought that the family that prays together stays together. As adults, it is a blessing that we have still held on to this time of prayer and praise, even though some of us are now living in different parts of the globe, some in England and some in the United States.

We look forward to meeting for our time of prayer and praise on Zoom, and our sessions also include a time of scintillating conversations about a selected topic and sharing our thoughts together. We have experienced many answers to prayer as we share together and unite and asking for God's leading in our lives.

There are interesting questions that are posed by the member who is nominated to chair for each week, and these are some of the answers that were shared by the family during one such session. We were challenged to share the lessons we will learn after the coronavirus pandemic has ended and how these lessons could be incorporated into our lives.

After the global pandemic is over, it would bring a sense of gratitude and praise for the fact that God had brought us through it and His ability to help us to maintain a sense of discipline and trust. Another view was that God can do anything and can use even technology at a time when the church doors were closed, which provided members with an alternative way of connecting with one another. This illustrates the caring nature of a God who is in control and is familiar with our basic need for fellowship. The importance of service to others in need was reinforced and would therefore reinforce our commitment to look out for others who are suffering through the loss of loved ones, loss of employment, and loss of housing.

One other member talked about the support aspect and how God can be praised for keeping us safe and enabling us to socially distance to save lives and control the virus. It would also be reflected as a time of self-denial and praising God for His gift of salvation in saving souls. Another lesson to be learned would be to reflect on God's provision of services, for example, food deliveries, delivery of prescription to those unable to go out, and other services that had been provided throughout the lockdown and other practical help from those who were willing to support the elderly and vulnerable in the community.

The faith element was noted as crucial to us all as a family and an awareness of the world and how needs were met from the social, physical, emotional, and mental health perspective. Faith therefore would be reflected on afterwards as playing an important role in lifting our voices in prayer and praise to the One who has been instrumental in bringing about a sense of peace and contentment amidst all the chaos of daily living.

Love was identified to be the basis and the reason for rejoicing and praising God for his sustained goodness, the family connectedness, and support that united us throughout the years, including the pandemic.

My personal reflection would be to value life as precious and not to take it for granted by taking one day at a time. In retrospect, after the virus has gone, it would reinforce the need to live a life of contentment and not shop for things that I do not need. It would be a time to continue my prayer life, and the lesson of showing compassion to those who are going through dark times would be beneficial.

Praise allows God's power to overcome circumstances no matter how desperate they may seem and maintains a contentment-centred way of life. We agreed that it will be a time to think about all the good and positive things that happened during the pandemic and how God was able to produce beauty out of ashes. Some of us were able to report new job opportunities, healing, and other good news that happened within the family.

It is always a time of thanksgiving when we have seen God working in miraculous ways in answering prayers on many levels and keeping us connected as a family.

21

PRAYER

Oh, that You would bless me indeed, and enlarge my
territory, that Your hand would be with me, and that You
would keep me from evil, that I may not cause pain.
1 Chronicles 4:10

Howow has the gift of prayer made a significant impact on your
daily life? Have you been called to a ministry of intercession for others?

One of the most significant desires of Jesus's disciples was to teach
them to pray, and from this request, the gift of prayer was given to
them and to us. The Lord's Prayer, as recorded in Matthew 6:9–13,
has been the most significant model for prayer gifted by our Lord. It
captures the tenet of Christian living, beginning with worship and
acknowledging who God is, giving full reverence to His name. It
follows a life pattern that recognises God as our Father and is an
expression of worship to him.

The Lord's Prayer acknowledges God's Holy Name and
sovereignty and asks for His will to be done. Praying for the necessities
of life, like bread, and avoidance of temptation are important elements
of the words that Jesus used. It relates to human relationships and
concludes by giving glory to God for His eternal kingdom and power.

From an early age, I was taught to pray and to ask for God's
blessings. It did not matter if the problem was great or small. It

meant a lot to me to attend mid-week prayer meetings. I would hear people pray long prayers as though they had a special and intimate relationship with God that I did not experience at that time.

As I grew older, prayer became a vital part of my life. I learned that the length of my prayers did not matter; the important thing was to begin and end the day with prayer, giving God the opportunity to bless and direct me.

I recognised prayer as a gifted channel of communication with God and a privilege to turn to Him at every point of need for decisions that I had to make as a young Christian. It meant thanking God for providing food, clothing, and everything else that I needed. It also provided an opportunity to bring every matter to God and express my concerns and thanksgiving to Him.

I wrote the poem 'My Mother's Bedside' many years ago when I reflected on the beautiful gift of prayer. Her prayers were intense; she had so much to say to the Lord. I admired her desire to linger in His presence.

Her practice of an open door to her bedroom led me to believe in the concept that God's door is always open and that He is attentive to our prayers. I began to unwrap this gift with a huge amount of gratitude and thanksgiving, with His presence being a close reality, especially in prayer. Prayer allowed me to experience answers through faith, believing that He can do so much more above everything that I desired. I began to believe in a God that is bigger than anything I can encounter in all the journeys of life.

Not all prayers were answered. At those times, it changed my attitude, which is essentially more important. It became a great part of worship and building a relationship with God that meant I could talk to Him about anything as my Heavenly Father, including intercessory prayers for others.

One of my prayers that involved waiting was the prayer to become a mother. I had lost my first child through a miscarriage early on in my marriage. I waited seven years for prayers to be answered. During that time, I relied on prayer and patience for the answer to be fulfilled. The answer finally came in 1977 at the birth of my daughter, and two years later, I had a son. God answered my prayer according to His will and timing and gave me not just one child but two. I now have three grandchildren, one of which is a great-granddaughter! Such is the nature of God's multiplication.

Prayer then became a gift that I treasure because it has helped my Christian faith to grow and mature. Although waiting has been a struggle at times, I have still found the personal and reflective outlet of expressing my thoughts to God to be a blessing. It uplifts a heavy heart as earnest prayers bring about changes. To call on the Lord's name is described in Scripture as a fortress for security from the unanswered questions in times of discouragement and disbelief.

It is important to make quality time with God a priority. It requires me to set a special time aside. It is the Christian's lifeline, so my commitment to begin the day in prayer has been a lifelong pattern. Finding a regular space in the home, without distractions is helpful, and a regular chair creates an atmosphere of reserved quiet time with the Lord.

I have found that if I neglect to do that or rush through a prayer while getting ready for work or other commitments, it has resulted in a less productive day. At the same time, when I commit the day to God, I find that even if I experience more problems, I can cope with them with a different mindset. Praying helps to overcome the obstacles.

The habit of keeping a prayer list will make your prayer session more specific and meaningful as you intercede for others. Prayer gives an avenue for confession and seeking forgiveness for what has been done that is not in harmony with His purpose. As His children, He has an interest in what happens to us and wants to be involved, so prayer is the key that unlocks His ability to work and intervene in situations that are difficult to manage.

The power of God's intervention came one day when I called a friend who had been very ill recently and was in hospital due to a spike in her diabetic levels and was treated with intravenous insulin to get her blood sugar levels under control. She has been suffering with quite a few other physical ailments, and this was part of a catalogue of symptoms that has made her feel very poorly.

She shared with me what has been happening in her health and how anxious and concerned she has been. I listened and shared my experience as a diabetic and offered to pray with her. Immediately after the prayer, her spirits lifted, and she began to claim God's power to heal and help her at this time. I could sense relief in her voice.

Prayer can have a powerful effect on our well-being and introduces a level of belief and trust in God who has the power to heal and restore us, irrespective of what the problem may be.

One of the benefits of prayer is the power that it gives to release hope, healing, and freedom with submission to His will. It brings an alignment with His plan through humility and simplicity. The gift of prayer is the Christian's tool that brings an alignment with God's ability to work on our behalf.

Jesus, as my example, went into the mountain to pray during His earthly ministry. He chose to come away from all the hustle and bustle because He recognised how crucial it was to be alone and in quiet solitude before His Father. His example teaches me that I need to find a time and place to focus on prayer and make it an important priority in my life. It is the life blood of the Christian who desires to know more about God's will and purpose and to delve more into God's plan.

Sometimes in praying for something, it may not always be the answer that you are looking for, but God has a million ways of working out His purposes as 'all things work together for good to those who love God, to those who are the called according to His purpose' (Romans 8:28).

Jesus prayed many times to the Father. He prayed for me. He prayed for His disciples as they were given the call to prepare them for the sharing of the Gospel. Jesus prayed when He was in the Garden of Gethsemane before His death. Jesus found prayer to be essential and admonished His followers to pray without ceasing and as a way of guarding against temptations because He knows that even in our willingness, the flesh is weak (Matthew 26:41).

The approach to prayer can come from a self-righteous motive of just wanting to prove how good we are rather than in humility and worship. An example of this is when two men went into the temple to pray (Luke 18:10). One of them, a Pharisee, boasted about how good he was and how glad he was that he was not a sinner and compared himself as better than other people. His pious words listed all the good things he had done, like fasting twice a week, and even looked down on the other man beside him, who was a tax collector.

The tax collector stood at a distance and quietly confessed that he was a sinner and asked for forgiveness. Jesus said that he had a better understanding of what righteousness is all about because he left the temple and went home 'justified'. Jesus concluded that those who exalt themselves will be humbled and those who humble themselves will be exalted (Luke 18:14).

There are many wonderful prayers in the Bible, and their principal purpose is to draw us closer to God and make a connection and communication with the Almighty. It is through the gift and channel of prayer that petitions are made, God's vision is revealed, and answers are given according to God's will.

A few years ago, I was given a gift of a book by one of my siblings, called *The Prayer of Jabez* by Bruce Wilkinson. It has been an amazing book, based on 1 Chronicles 4, that focuses on Jabez's prayer. Wilkinson said that it distils God's powerful will for our future with many gifts that are unclaimed.

Jabez had a better reputation than his brothers, and it was out of pain that his mother had conceived him (1 Chronicles 4:9). His prayer was that God would enlarge his territory and give him a double portion of blessings. He knew that the secret to his success depended on prayer, the greatest arsenal in the spiritual battle against the enemy. Jabez's desire was that God would protect him from harm. Judah had been under siege due to disobedience. They had lost God's protection by wanting their own way and had become unfaithful to God. Through this beautiful prayer, Jabez sought God's protection from harm.

There are some essential lessons which I researched from Jabez's prayer that are worth considering. Jabez recognised God's lordship over his life. He cried out to God. His prayer for God to bless him was from a heart that was fully invested in God's blessings. Jabez asked God to multiply his influence and grant him blessing through His leading. He was aware of his vulnerability and prayed for God's intervention against the enemy.

Based on my experience, prayer is essentially a way of spending quality time with God in quietness and humility, as His will becomes clearer. It can be in single solitude or as a group. It can be silent or openly expressed. It gives an opportunity to intercede for others and to ask for His blessing and resist the tendency to limit God according to limited understanding. It is also a time of confession, rededication, rejoicing, and praising, which builds hope and power to deal with life's challenges.

Many times, prayer requires the challenge of waiting, and there may also be times when prayers are not answered. It enables and empowers faith in the outworking of answers, which may not always give instantaneous and positive answers.

There are many benefits to prayer that help us to unwrap God's promises of love and faithfulness as we release our cares to Him. It allows a time to be sensitive to what He wants as the Holy Spirit guides and inspires in accordance with His perfect purpose.

Prayers need not be elaborate. Even the simplicity of a child's prayers can be quite powerful. The psalmist David referred to an all-knowing God in Psalm 139, recognising that He already knows our thoughts and searches our hearts, so there's no need to impress Him with our prayers, like the one offered by the pharisee mentioned earlier on. The more prayer is offered up, the more power is given to overcome.

I have found many benefits to prayer, including victory and healing of the sick (James 5:15). Faith is accompanied by persistent prayers when asking, seeking, and knocking which can make all the difference. I have found the gift of prayer to have many specific benefits:

- Prayer invites the Holy Spirit to intercede.
- Prayer releases power to overcome temptation.
- Prayer gives protection throughout the day.
- Prayer provides a panacea for inner turmoil that I may be feeling as I acknowledge a greater power than myself to handle situations.
- Through the channel of prayer, I gain a closer relationship with Him as the channels of communication are kept open through consistent prayer (Crosswalk.com).

When thinking of the fact that prayer invites the Holy Spirit's presence to intercede came one wintry morning when I woke up to find that the snow had been falling quite heavily overnight. I was not aware of it and was surprised to look out in the morning and see the whole of my street covered.

The once green grassy areas, and as far as I could see, were now completely covered with a blanket of snow. Although it was beautiful to look out on, I knew that I had to go out and was reluctant to drive as I might skid and I would lose control of my car. Skidding in the snow had happened before, and the memory of that experience put me in the position of not wanting to repeat the frightening episode again.

As I walked along the path to the shops, I began to pray for my safety along the treacherous road. I saw children playing cheerfully in the snow with no reservation of falling, and in fact, falling was all part of the fun as they rode along on skates and tried to compete with their friends. On the other hand, I was walking gingerly along, taking special care not to fall. Before long, I did fall, and thankfully, a kind gentleman came to my rescue and helped me back on my feet again. I felt helpless and embarrassed about the experience, but someone had been there to give me a hand, so I didn't suffer any major injury.

The prayer of Jabez—'O that you would bless me'—was a great encouragement to remember the help that is available from our loving Heavenly Father when we fall. He is on hand to turn our sins into something that is similar to untouched, untrodden, and spotless snow. I'm glad that there is no sin that is too tainted for His cleansing power to transform and no fall so deep that He cannot rescue and reinstate me back on my feet again. Through prayer, I received His protection that day.

The beneficial gift of prayer leads me into a time where I can talk to God, the ruler of the universe! My Father loves me and invites me to come and talk to Him so that we can both listen to each other. It builds on my relationship with Him and knowing that He already knows my needs makes it easy to come to Him in prayer.

I agree that it then gives me the opportunity to see it from His perspective rather than mine, as I can easily get caught up in how problems are affecting me rather than what His will is and how He can turn it around to my highest good. Prayer allows me to change my attitude to the problem by recognising His will to be done rather than mine.

A few years ago, I visited the United States of America for a holiday to visit my family in California. We spent one day travelling to Yosemite National Park, which was the first time for me. This was such an amazing experience.

As we drove higher up the winding paths of the beautiful mountain, I looked down and admired the tall stately trees and forests. The magnificent landscape was truly breathtaking. As we reached Yosemite Park, we had time to stop and look around, take photographs, and have lunch. It was such an experience of beauty as we enjoyed God's creation and reflected on how lovely the world is when we go a little higher and reach the summit.

Prayer for me is like ascending the mountains when I talk to God. It is like going up that special place of solitude, just as Jesus did to be still and reflect and see things from a different vantage point. Prayer gives a new perspective on my journey as I unwrap this beautiful gift.

22

SECOND CHANCES

In what ways have you received a second chance, and how do you deal with the challenges of life?

It was during the year 1987 that I experienced the end of my marriage. It was an incredibly stressful and problematic season in my life. When I realised that the marriage had irretrievably broken down, I knew I had to make some drastic changes and decisions. I needed God to step in and extend His hand of grace to me as I had lost my home, my friends, my money, and my job. I had lost everything at that point.

I remember the physical and emotional trauma that I experienced at that time. I needed a second chance at life and regain my belief in myself and in God. I had to put the disappointment of a failed marriage behind me, and I recalled God's goodness. He was my refuge and rock at that time. I was in desperate need of His protection on my life and my future.

I began by building a new circle of good friends, most of whom I had lost due to the divorce. These comprised new Christian friends and work colleagues, and practical support from my family who assisted in the road to recovery. It was the grace of God that intervened and extended His everlasting arms around me which I needed as a sign of reassurance of His love for me. He helped me to regain all the losses and provided me with a new future as I stepped out of my season of sad experience and into a purposeful life.

Through this disappointment, I have developed a more empathic attitude towards others who are going through loss of one kind or another and appreciating that life is transitory and precious. It has helped me to forge ahead, knowing that second chances are miracles whenever they come.

The decision to maintain personal values and hold on to self-respect are important choices to gain a fresh start. It was through the grace of God that we are able to accept this gift of second chances.

The unwrapping of this gift came in various stages. I had to firstly accept the experience of divorce as something—although in my experience, unplanned—to be an opportunity for learning more about myself. God gave me a second chance to allow Him to take control of my life, and by taking responsibility for my actions, I became more confident and resilient.

Benjamin Franklin was an American scientist, politician, inventor, and businessman. He once said that pain brings its own opportunities for learning, and that is what I planned to do. Through that experience, these are some of the lessons I learned.

The story of Ruth is a fascinating example of second chances and how God can extend grace out of a sad situation and make something beautiful out of it. It is recorded in the book of Ruth and brings encouragement and hope to me.

Ruth's experience happened at the time when the judges ruled and a famine had struck the land. Ruth's father-in-law, Elimelech and his wife, Naomi, made a journey from Bethlehem, Judah, to live in Moab, which is Jordan today. Elimelech and Naomi had two sons, Mahlon and Chilion, who married two women from Moab named Orpah and Ruth.

Tragedy struck the family when Naomi's husband died, and then both their two sons died also, leaving all three women as widows. Naomi felt that the only solution was for them to separate from one another as there were no other sons for them to marry, Naomi said and spoke to Orpah and Ruth.

Orpah agreed to go back to her people, but Ruth did not want to part from Naomi, her mother-in-law. She pleaded with her, saying, 'Entreat me not to leave you or to turn back from following after you; for wherever you go I will go, and wherever you lodge I will lodge; your people shall be my people and your God my God' (Ruth 1:16).

Naomi and Ruth went back to Bethlehem together, while Orpah made her choice to go back home to her people and country.

During this time, Ruth experienced a change of events when she met Naomi's wealthy relative Boaz and got married, having a son named Obed from the marriage. Obed was then the son of Jesse and the son of David, the line through which Jesus came!

Ruth had lost her husband and the chance of getting children, and in that culture, she would have been scorned not only as a widow but also a childless one. It was from famine to feast as she enjoyed the wealth of Boaz, who found her, who gave her a second chance at happiness.

> From a life of barrenness, Ruth experienced the blessing of giving birth to a son, a second chance to experience raising her own family, and from her pain of widowhood came a life of wedded bliss. She became the wife of a wealthy man who had everything to offer her to compensate for the loss of her husband and family.

I resonate with the prayer of Ruth as she pleaded to her mother-in-law not to separate from her. I felt those words of 'Entreat me not to leave You" (Ruth 1:16). The gift of second chances came as I embraced a new and positive decision to begin the journey of new choices and rebuilding my life.

The element of faith in God enabled Ruth to see that the gift of second chances meant that God was not finished with her. The continuing work of refinement and purpose is a gift worth holding on to, and you never know where it will lead to. It does not matter what life throws at you. It is reassuring to know that life is not over for the one who is willing to believe in fortitude and blessing through faithfulness. You can begin again!

There are some outstanding qualities I found in Ruth; one of which was her loyalty as a daughter-in-law who obeyed Naomi and followed her advice. Most important of all was her decision to accept Naomi's faith and believe in God for herself. She had put God first, and all the other things were given to her by the gift of grace through second chances.

23

TRUST IN GOD

Trust in the Lord with all your heart and lean
not on your own understanding; in all your ways
acknowledge Him and He shall direct your paths.
Proverbs 3:5,6

How did you begin the journey of trusting in God? Has it been a process of experiential growth?

The above verse instructs us to trust in the Lord because when we do so, He is able to give us direction in life and not lead us astray and down some paths that are dangerously harmful.

There are many things in life that require implicit trust. For instance, we have to trust those who prepare our food in a restaurant or the pilot on the plane whose credentials we may never be able to verify. What about the taxi driver whose licence to drive is not seen and his knowledge of our journey is never questioned? We rely on the assumption that he knows the route sufficiently to take you to your destination in the quickest and safest way possible.

The word *trust* has a special connotation because it embodies the idea of reliability. In order to trust someone, there must be trustworthiness and dependability. It is the bedrock of any relationship that is meaningful, and the gift of trust is ever unfolding as reliance on God becomes greater through getting to know Him and trusting Him.

The idea of leaning on your own understanding is considered by Solomon to be the avoidance of doubting God's wisdom and taking Him at face value for what He has said. In today's world, there are many reasons for distrust as there are so many failed promises, misused guarantees, and let-downs that cause you to be wary of what people say and what they mean. These two must be synonymous with each other, but in many cases, they are not. We are left with the choice to second-guess and lean on our own understanding.

One of the great biblical examples of implicit trust was demonstrated by Abraham, who implicitly followed God's leading. Abraham and his wife, Sarah, had waited many long years for a son. Abraham had been promised to be the father of many nations. His name was changed from Abram to Abraham when God made a covenant between them (Genesis 17:2,4,6).

The promise of a family did not come to fruition until he and Sarah were quite old, and she was past childbearing years, so the promise of being a father of nations must have seemed remote, to say the least. Trust sometimes means reaching out in the dark when you can't see all the answers in front of you.

Although God had made a promise to Abraham, he tried to short-circuit God's plans when Sarah suggested that their servant Hagar should bear a child for him. Hagar had a son who was named Ishmael. Hagar then had to run away because of discord that developed between Hagar and Sarah afterwards. The time then came for the announcement that Abraham and Sarah would now be blessed with a son and heir. He was named Isaac and was to become Abraham's promised heir.

Having the gift of trust means understanding God's impeccable timing. Abraham was then told by God to go to a land called Moriah and sacrifice his son Isaac there (Genesis 22:2). This must have been a total reversal of what Abraham was promised as Isaac represented the beginning of the inheritance. Yet God's timing is perfect when trust is permitted to become the basis of the relationship. He had to obey the voice of God, in total trust that it would work out in the end.

God provided another opportunity for Abraham to demonstrate his trust in Him by asking Abraham to sacrifice his son. Just before he was about to do so, Abraham heard a voice, saying, 'Do not lay your hand on the lad, or do anything to him; for now I know that you fear God since you have not withheld your son, your only son, from Me' (Genesis 22:12).

In surrender and trust, Abraham realised that God would either raise up another son afterwards or make some other provision when he said to the young men with him, 'Stay here with the donkey, the lad and I will go yonder, and worship and we will come back to you' (Genesis 22:5).

He exercised total reliance on God and refused to doubt Him, and a lamb was provided in the thicket so that Abraham was able to use it as a sacrifice instead of his son. There is no disappointment outside of His ability to carry out His promises, even if it doesn't make sense at the time.

> Trusting in God gives the power to move forward in surrender. A total trust in His timing means that I must wait, like Abraham, for the promise to unfold, without questioning. All it takes is for patience and a change of attitude so that God can help you to surmount the difficulty.

When confronted with unwelcoming situations, the gift of trust helps to adopt a daring attitude. It does not cloud your vision of reality, nor can it be regarded as the weak option. It gives strength to face the attack of pessimism and fear and empowers the individual to continue to live a life of contentment and faith.

Being able to trust in God comes with a sense of maturity as the relationship grows and deepens. It is a gift the strengthens the Christian's belief and is the power that brings us to Christ in the first place. It is only when trust is placed in Jesus Christ and what He did to save us that we are given absolution from sin and brought into a solid relationship with Him by faith.

When going through the ordeal of suffering, it is hard to imagine a good outcome because it can be an overpowering experience, which brings a sense of aloneness and despair. Trusting God when going through loss and other painful circumstances can be a challenge. At the same time, it is trust that helps to unleash the power to cope and overcome in Jesus's name.

I began the journey of developing trust as I started out on the path of experiences that propelled me into trusting God for the little as well as the big things in my life. The gift of trust was important when I was faced with a problem that was too difficult to handle on my own. My relationship with God then developed through daily meditation, prayer, and regular Bible study. I found memorising texts beneficial and motivated me to get to know Him more as a God of love.

I discovered that the gift of faith works hand in hand with trust. You do not immediately see the outcome, but trust helps you to believe. It begins with tiny baby steps and is a precious way of handling situations and gaining favourable results. At the time when I was less focused on trusting the God of circumstances, the time eventually came when I prayed into my acceptance of this gift.

There are many things in life that can cause us to be troubled and concerned. These are difficult times that we are living in, and it is hard sometimes to implicitly trust in an invisible God or have the confidence to know the path where He is leading. It is at these times that trust is needed to hold on to His promises, like Abraham did.

At one stage in my life, I recall doors being shut, and I was in total confusion as to what was going on. I was filled with disappointment because the job I had applied for ended in rejection causing a brief time of unemployment. Short-term employment did not become long-term. I wondered what I was doing wrong. My faith was at an all-time low, and I experienced one disappointment after another. The debts were mounting. I didn't understand the reason for what I was going through. I cried out to the Lord, and faith began to help me to place my trust in Him that everything would be resolved.

Things began to change when permission is given to accept that there would be an improvement eventually. Faith becomes a coping mechanism that allows us to be free, to find a way out and think clearly and creatively. As one door closes, substitute doors are opened so that provision is always made at the right time.

When in prayer, I believe that God is aware of the issue, but is waiting for me to bring it to Him in an attitude of belief. At that point, He begins to work through answered prayer, because exercising faith is the only way of gaining His good pleasure. 'Without faith it is impossible to please Him' (Hebrews 11:6). This is not only a placation but also a reassurance that God can be trusted to work on my behalf.

Trusting God may take time and means letting go in full surrender. This may place us in an awkward, vulnerable position. As humans, we like to be in control. The consolation to treasure is that God can be trusted to take us through whatever challenges lie ahead of us, regardless of the valley or season we are in.

24

Service to Others

As each one has received a gift, minister it to one another,
as good stewards of the manifold grace of God.
1 Peter 4:10

How has the gift of service to others brought satisfaction? Are there specific areas where you feel led to become a volunteer?

Service to others is a special gift that begins with a compassionate heart. It is a selfless act of kindness that reaches out to others who are in need, whether in the local community or on a global scale. This is the ultimate reward that this gift brings as stewards of everything we have.

It is always a heart-warming story that inspires others who witness humanitarian work around the world and at home, who display a genuine charitable responsibility that everyone ought to have.

The gift of giving in service to others involves time, ability, and material possessions of sharing what you have with those less fortunate than ourselves. It is a voluntary response to dire needs around us. Giving and sharing are a part of the service that is required in reaching out and finding out where there are needs that can be filled by us in some way.

The gift is received as an act of worship and humanitarian response that brings satisfaction through humble efforts to bring happiness into other people's lives. One example is the service of

Mother Teresa, as she met the needs of her community. Born in the nineteenth century, she dedicated her life to those living in Calcutta, India. She unwrapped the gift of service to those who were in need and won the Nobel Peace Prize for her humanitarian devotion to others. She had a love for people, and her mission of service, which happened at an early age, motivated her to open a hospice for disabled and aged people and a leper colony.

An account of the life of an inspirational and industrious woman is mentioned in the Book of Acts 9:36–42. Within these verses, I recognise a woman with an incredible gift of service to others. She is best known as Dorcas, which is an interpretation of her other name as Tabitha. Dorcas lived in Joppa and was known for her acts of kindness. She made clothes for widows and was respected and loved by her community. When she died, the entire community mourned her death as a great loss of someone who selflessly devoted her life to the gift of service to others.

A miracle took place in the end when Peter was able to restore her to life. Peter went to the upper room where all the women were mourning her loss. Peter said a prayer and then said the words 'Tabitha, arise'. She sat up and opened her eyes, and hand in hand with Peter, she got up and joined the others. Many were saved as a result (Acts 9:39–42).

In 2013, I was invited to join two of my siblings to become part of a large missionary project being held in Los Angeles, United States of America. I did not hesitate in accepting the invitation to be involved in missionary work. When I agreed to go on this mission trip, I had no idea how large it would be and the impact it would have on the community in Los Angeles and my contribution to its success. I accepted the challenge in faith to support the project.

Pathway to Health, as it was called, gave me an opportunity to sacrifice time and energy into the success of the huge project. It was a giant collaborative endeavour with the aim of reaching hundreds of people who had no health care and needed urgent medical attention, which was free of charge.

I was assigned to work in the Patient Registration department as a volunteer as part of a large team who assisted in welcoming the public as they entered the building. There were many qualified doctors, nurses, surgeons, dentists who volunteered their time and expertise to be involved in this work of service to others in need. I was also able to talk and pray with the visitors as they walked in with their registration forms.

It was a humbling experience to be part of a work that involved the Adventist Laymen's Services and Industries, Adventist Health (specifically Glendale Adventist Medical Center, White Memorial Medical Center, and Simi Valley Medical Center), Loma Linda University, Seventh-Day Adventist Church, and Southern California Conference.

The gift of serving others at that event involved prayer sessions. It was important to greet people in a warm, welcoming and loving way. One of the requests that we were asked to pray about was for God's will to be done in all the logistics for this event and for His name to be lifted high. I can honestly say that this was achieved. I greeted families and those who attended on their own, all of whom had queued up for hours from early in the morning to be examined by a doctor and given free medical attention.

We shared love as a witness to those desperately in need of it. One woman, as she came to my station, remarked on the love and acceptance that she felt by everyone and asked, 'Is this a church? I thought so because everyone is smiling and full of love.'

The whole event was very well organised, and there was a level of unity amongst all the volunteers who made it special. During my experience of the Pathway to Health event, I found listening to be important to those who are hurting.

There are many ways that we can help on different levels to meet the emotional, physical, and social needs of those around us and farther afar. I felt privileged to recognise the role that God had given me to bless others in this way.

> And the King will answer and say to them 'Assuredly,
> I say to you inasmuch as you did it to one of the least of
> these My brethren, you did it to Me. (Matthew 25:40)

The needs of those at home and globally are becoming greater and greater. Yet there are some who hesitate to contribute to helping others live a better quality of life. The known maxim 'Charity begins at home' was a phrase quoted by an ex-boss who was reluctant to donate towards a worthy cause when I approached him one day during an ingathering campaign run by the church. He held tightly to his pockets and decided to reject the opportunity to show mercy and compassion to the less fortunate.

There are volunteer organisations that support those who are in need within our community. It is my Christian duty to play a part in this and to do whatever I can to join in service to others through giving in whatever way I am impressed to do.

> The gift of service to others enables anyone and everyone to be available and involved in reaching out and looking for practical ways to serve. The challenge is to become more sensitively aware by discovering spiritual gifts that lead to kind and helpful ways to support other people. It may come through the auspices of the local church community or as an individual calling like Mother Teresa.

Jesus gave the example of how this gift could be used to evangelise the world through love and humility. The idea of 'giving something back' is part of it, but very often it is simply an appreciation for what you are able to do to help someone else, whose situation in life may have been caused by a particular season of poverty or the result of a natural disaster that has taken place.

There are many organisations and groups that devote time and resources in responding to the poor, the hungry, and the homeless. Their gift of service to others is commended and is an invitation to all to become involved in the service to others that Jesus requires as true religion.

The reason for the gifts we are given reflect the heart of the Giver. He is concerned about the way our gifts are used in a loving way, with the right motives. The motives must be pure with a genuine desire to reach out and be the loving touch of a powerful healing endeavour.

Jesus provided a mission-centred approach that identified needs, whether physical or spiritual, that brought wholesomeness and healing to a dying world. He fed the hungry and healed the sick and miraculously touched the lives of everyone who met Him with love and concern for their condition. The mandate to us is that in using the gift of service to others, we are effectively serving Him.

26

INNER RENEWAL

For by grace you have been saved through faith, and
that not of yourselves, it is the Gift of God.
Ephesians 2:8

Have you received the gift of new life? What difference has this
change made in your life since accepting the gift of inner renewal?

The search for inner renewal or conversion, as is usually called,
was experienced by an Ethiopian man as his saving faith brought
grace that resulted in a changed life. This gift of renewal came for
the Ethiopian who immediately accepted the Gospel and asked to
be baptised when he said, 'What hinders me from being baptised?'
(Acts 8:26–40).

He had a high position, in charge of all the treasury, and worked
for the queen of the Ethiopians, named Candace. On this occasion,
he came to Jerusalem to worship and was sitting in a chariot reading
the Bible from the prophet Isaiah, but he didn't understand what he
was reading. Led by the Holy Spirit, Philip joined him to explain what
he was reading and had a Bible study, after which he requested to be
baptised there and then.

Like the Ethiopian man, I was once faced with a similar decision
about the question of what my hindrance is to being baptised. It
happened on a beautiful day in December 1990, that I felt a sense

of renewal on the day of my recommitment through baptism. I was first baptised when I was in my teens at a revival campaign and felt the call of God then and became a Seventh-Day Adventist Christian after re-baptism.

Since that time, the process of renewal has been a journey of anticipation of what God can do in developing the gift of renewal. Amidst all the ups and downs, I have experienced His power of renewal every time I wake up and greet a new day. I feel refreshed and transformed on the inside when I commit the day in prayer to God and claim His forgiveness and cleansing power.

This gift of inner renewal comes packaged in salvation, which is a free and universal gift. It is not an exclusive gift that only some can afford but can be unwrapped by the poorest as well as the richest, irrespective of whatever station in life we find ourselves.

> The gift of renewal is lasting and everlasting, given alongside mercy. The gift is not imposed but rather is dependent on the one who is willing to receive it graciously. It is a special gift that only God can give because He knows our need of Him, and our true character and our resolve to serve Him then become evident.

For this reason, I love attending baptismal services. It demonstrates the gift of renewal that has taken place in someone's life. One such baptism took place at a Seventh-Day Adventist Church in North London. There were three candidates, and one of them was the daughter of someone I had not long ago made friends with. She invited me to come and witness the happy occasion and share one of my poems called 'Calvary Love'. She had heard me sharing it on a previous occasion at one of our church services and loved it and felt it would be a blessing for her daughter to hear it as well on this occasion.

I arrived at the church that Sabbath afternoon, in plenty of time as I was keen to witness this ceremony and to see the happy faces of the three candidates. My poem was well received, and their testimonies were very inspiring. Their faces were radiant as they all gave an account of what had happened to them on their journey of faith and renewal when they accepted Jesus Christ as their Lord and Saviour. I was impressed by their strong resolve, and my friend's daughter

said that she may never get married, but for her, this was the best
'marriage' she could hope for.

The gift of inner renewal had made all the difference to these
three young ladies' converted lives, and as far as they were concerned,
they had experienced the feeling of being loved and accepted that day
as they stepped out in faith. It was a faith that was small, like the tiny
mustard seed, and grew.

Jesus said that faith only needs to start as small as a mustard seed.
Of course, the mustard seed, once planted on good soil, must grow,
so my faith must not remain the same size year after year. My faith
ought to be growing.

The consequence of sin is death because of our naturally sinful
nature. In accepting the free gift of salvation, it gives renewal and
transformation that brings the promise of eternal life. Accepting the
undeniable truth brought contentment and a new beginning to these
ladies who accepted the opportunity to become new.

> Whatever the circumstances surrounding our Call,
> and the events that bring us to the point of receiving
> Salvation, I believe that everything is possible when
> confronted with the challenge to become new.

My transformational change came through obedience and the
desire to follow Him. As a new creation, I accepted the challenge
to walk by faith, believing that He could help me to keep the
commandments and live the life that He had designed for me all along.

The step was initially one that I had to consider, but in thinking it
through, the final decision was more purposeful and crucial. Following
Christ has to be an inner transaction of the heart where fellowship
becomes significant, as anything else is peripheral and transient.

26

CONCLUDING THOUGHTS

I love unwrapping gifts whether the gift is given to me, or I share in the joy of someone else unwrapping theirs. There is such a lovely feeling that someone has thought of something that you would like and appreciate. The cost and the size of the gift does not matter, it is the thought that counts. I really appreciate the thought that has gone into it.

The intention to please someone else really makes their day. The thoughtfulness brings happiness and a smiling response of thanks. It may be a total surprise, and this adds to the pleasure of receiving the gift. When words are not enough to say how we feel a gift may demonstrate love and good wishes. Whether or not we recognise it every one of us has been given a gift or a variety of gifts for the journey as we travel through life and its myriad of experiences. Some gifts are intangible like peace, prayer, hope and love, which are what this book relates to, and others are more tangible like the skill of becoming an artist or musician.

We are unique and the gifts that can be unwrapped are part and parcel of the blessings that are always available everyday of our lives given by a God who wants us to accept these gifts and enrich our lives through each and every season that we encounter.

The gift of a healthy lifestyle is a challenge to honour the body that has been given, and the gift of peace has a transforming stillness through the seasons as they present themselves. I cherish the gift of faith that helps me to see beyond what is happening and builds assurance and hope for the future.

The challenge to find forgiveness and reparation of broken relationships is found in the realisation of my own need for forgiveness. This has only been achieved through prayer in seeking my own divine healing. This has been a journey of faith believing that it is possible to let go and allow God to heal the brokenness.

Despite appearances, there is always hope that is gifted to those who want to develop trust and have a positive mindset within the context of contentment. These are the ones who accept the importance of self-worth and who use every opportunity to help others who are struggling with a low self-image through neglect or other issues. The satisfaction that comes through service to others is gratifying. This is one of the best definitions of experiencing success, and in the middle of helping others, we find second chances that rebuild and develop our own inner renewal.

All the gifts that are mentioned in "Gifts for your seasons" are waiting to be unwrapped through the grace of God. It is a daily choice to utilise the gifts as a way of navigating the seasons in your life. It is a means of becoming focused on the blessings as the Holy Spirit helps in discovering God's plan as the best way of tapping into the gifts every day.

I remain inspired by the examples of how God has worked with Bible characters mentioned in "Gifts for your seasons". They have been a source of encouragement as I reflect on the happiness of accepting the gifts that are freely ours. Like a parent wanting the best for his/her child, God wants to provide evidence of His love through the gifts that are accepted by faith. It promotes trust and encourages reliance on Him to show how best these gifts can be used and shared.

27

MY MOTHER'S BEDSIDE

I remember the things my mother said.
We would sit for hours beside her bed.
I felt I could talk to her about anything.
Whatever the problem, she'd let her heart sing.
She knew how to turn things over to God.
The Bible was always paged at His Word,
Where she found strength and support
To take her through each day, to comfort.
She was never perturbed by daily alarm.
Her faith was strong, protected from harm.
She understood the path of Christian walk.
For the Master, she'd witness and talk.
She shared experiences to help me grow.
At these times, she'd let me know
Whatever God's plan came into my life,
The battle was God's against all strife.
When she died, I sat at her bedside.
Gripped with grief and loss, I cried.
I loved by my mother's bedside to pray,
Remembering the best way to start the day!

Eudora Louise Oxley
18.02.17 − 14.07.2003

REFERENCES

Andrea Bocelli—songs, wife, and sons [biography]'. https://www.biography.com/musician/andrea-bocelli.

Arkless, J. (1983). *No Meat for Me Please!: Recipes for the Vegetarian in the Family*. Surrey, UK: Elliott Right Way Books.

Armand, M. R. (2020). 'Finding Godly Contentment and Overcoming the Need for Seeking Approval'. Butterfly Living. https://butterflyliving.org/finding-godly-contentment/. Accessed 13 Aug. 2021.

Bennett, R. T. (2016). *The Light in the Heart: Inspirational Thoughts for Living Your Best Life*. London, UK: Summerdale Publishers Limited.

Brand, P., and P. Yancey (1980). *Fearfully and Wonderfully Made*. Michigan, USA: Zondervan.

Brooks-Welch, M. (1957). The Touch of The Master's Hand. Brethren Press., U.S.A

Brown, J. (2019). 'Parenting Styles: Types of Effective Parenting Explained'. FindMyKidsBlog.Education.

Cartright, D. P. (2008). *A History of Movement and Ideas: What Is Peace?* UK: Cambridge University Press.

Chaffer, Fonda Cordis, I. N. Watts, et al. (1998). *This Quiet Place*. Review & Herald Publishing Association.

Christensen, C. M. (2010). *On Managing Yourself*. USA: Harvard Business School Corporation.

Covey, S. M. R., and R. R. Merrill (2008). *The Speed of Trust: The One Thing That Changes Everything*. UK: Simon & Schuster.

Davis, B., and T. Barnard (2003). *Defeating Diabetes: A No-Nonsense Approach to Type 2 Diabetes and the Diabesity Epidemic*. USA: Healthy Living Publications.

Day, G. 'What Is the Difference between Talents and Spiritual Gifts?' www.christianity.com/wiki/christian-life/difference-between-talent-and-spiritual-gifts.html.

De Liser, R. (2012). *The Credit Crunch Christian: 27 Ways to Look Up When Things Are Looking Down*. Europe: Autumn House Publishing.

Ehrmann, M. (1927). *Desiderata: Words for Life*.

Greene, A. 8 Surprising Heath Benefits of love. Woman's Day.

Groberg, D H. The Race. Sourcebooks Inc.

Hamilton, R. (2014). 'Why Children Need Love to Grow'. Using Science to Inspire (blog).

Hourly History (2017). Rosa Parks. The woman who ignited a movement.

Jeffers, S. (2007). *Feel the Dear and Do It Anyway*. UK: Vermillion.

Jeremiah, D. (2001). *Slaying the Giants in Our Life: You Can Win the Battle and Live Victoriously*. Nashville, TN, USA: W. Publishing Group.

MacArthur, J. (1993, 2012). *Anxious for Nothing. God's Cure for the Cares of Your Soul*. UK: David C. Cook, Kingsway Communications.

Mandella, N.R. (2006). Mandella: The Authorized Portrait. Andrews McMeel Publishing, LLC, Kansas City, USA

Massey, P (2010). The parable of the two debtors in modern terms. The Biola University. Chimes newpaper.com

Oxley, P. (2009). *Beyond the Valley*. UK: Authorhouse UK Limited.

Pierce, T. (2012). 'Health and Wealth' (poem). www.poemhunter.com.

Ponton, L. (2016). 'What Is Forgiveness?' PsychCentral.com.

Pope, A. *An Essay on Criticism, Part II.* 1London, UK: Scholar Press.

Seaglove, I. (2000). *The Write Mood.* Kansas City, MO, USA: Andrews McMeel.

Sequeira, J. (1993). *Beyond Belief: The Promise, the Power, and the Reality of the Everlasting Gospel.* Nampa, Idaho: Pacific Press Publishing Association.

The Holy Bible. New King James Version (1998). USA: Thomas Nelson Inc.

Tozer, A. W. (1993). The Pursuit of God: The Human Thirst for the Divine. Camphill, PA. USA: Wing Spread Publishers.

Walker, A. (2011). The color purple. New ed. Orion. Phoenix

White, E. G. (2002). The Desire of Ages. Thou Canst Make Me Clean. Ch 27. Nampa, Idaho: Pacific Press.

White, E. G. (2010). The Great Controversy. Vermont, TN: Harvestime.

White, E. G. My Life Today, 95, 96.

Wilcox, E. W. The Set of the Sails: A Self-Esteem Poem. EllenBailey.com. Accessed 25 Apr. 2021.

Wilkinson, B., and D. Kopp (2000). The Prayer of Jabez: Breaking through to the Blessed Life. USA: Mulnomah Publishers Inc.

Winfrey, O. (2014). What I Know for Sure, 179. New York City, USA: Macmillan.

Links

Johnson, S. (2006). 'The Fountain of Content Must Spring Up in the Mind . . .'. Wildmind. Accessed 29 Jun. 2021.

Ehrmann, Max. *Desiderata: Words for Life.* https://www.wildmind. org/blogs/quote-of-the-month/quote-samuel-johnson-contentment. Accessed 14 Jun. 2021.

https://bible.knowing-jesus.com/topics/The-Gifts-Of-God. Accessed 23 Jul. 2021.

BBC Future. 'How Does Your Voice Box Work?' https://bbc.com/ future/aticle/20160506. Accessed 4 Jul. 2021.

'What Is Peace?' Bing images. Accessed 20 Apr. 2021.

https//www.georgemuller.org/a-famous-story-about-mullers' faith. Accessed 27 Aug. 2021.

'Parenting Styles: Types of Effective Parenting Explained'. FindMyKids Blog. Accessed 28 Aug. 2021.

Lockwood Huie, J. 'Forgiveness Quotes and Sayings: Quotes about Forgiveness'. JonathanLockwoodHuie.com. Accessed 23 Sep. 2021.

Keller, Helen. 'Hope Sees the Invisible, Feels the Intangible, and Achieves the Impossible'. Quotes.net. Accessed 26 Sep. 2021.

Rosa Parks Facts. The Mother of Civil Rights
Biography of Rosa Parks | Rosa Parks Facts

BIBLICAL REFERENCES

Introduction	Matthew 7:11; Luke 12:32; 1 Corinthians 12:4
My Moher's Bible	2 Peter 1:21; 2 Timothy 3:16; Isaiah 41:10; 2 Timothy 2:15.
Contentment	1 Timothy 6:10; Luke 12:20; Matthew 19:16, 22; Philippians 4:6,12, 19
Courage	Genesis 15:1; Genesis 26:24; Numbers 13:18–20; Numbers 14:7–9; 2 Timothy 1:7
Creation	Genesis 2:20; John 1:4–6; Genesis 3:5; Isaiah 40:28; Psalm 37:5
Faith	Jeremiah 17:7–8; Matthew 8:5–13; Revelation 22:13; Psalm 37:5
Forgiveness	Luke 23:34; Matthew 18:21–35; Colossians 3:13
Friendships	Proverbs 18:24; Job 1:1; Job 2:9, 12; Job 19:25–26; Job 42:10, 12; 1 Samuel 18:7
Gratitude	Psalm 68:19; Luke 17:13, 17; Psalm 33:1; Psalm 136:1

God's love   James 1:17; John 3:16

Healing   Genesis 25:7, 3; John 1:2; Matthew 8:5-13

Hope   Luke 24:21, 32, 35; Jeremiah 29:11;

Hospitality   Hebrews 13:2; Luke 10:38–42; 2 Samuel 9;
                      John 6:4, 9; Romans 12:13

Inner Renewal   Ephesians 2:18; Acts 8:26–40

Love   Jeremiah 31:3; Hosea 14; 1 Corinthians 13;
                      Lamentations 3:22, Hosea 1:2, 9, Hosea 9:10

Opportunity   Luke 19:10, 5

Parenting   Luke 15:11–32; Psalm 127:3

Peace   John 14:27; John 16:33; Mark 4:39; Philippians
                      4:7; Colossians 3:15; Isaiah 30:15

Praise   Psalm 33:1; Acts 16:28; Acts 16: 7, 9

Prayer   1 Chronicles 4:10, 9; Matthew 26:41; Matthew
                      6:9–13; Luke 18:10, 14; Romans 8:28; James
                      5:15; Psalm 139

Success   Genesis 37:7, 9; Genesis 50:20; Acts 16:7, 9;
                      Acts 16:7

Second Chances   Ruth 1:16

Service to Others   Matthew 25:40; Acts 9:36–42; 1 Peter 4:10

Self-Worth   Matthew 10:29–31; Hebrews 2:7; Psalm 8:4;
                      Song of Solomon 2:4; Psalm 139:14; John 4:15,
                      John 3:16

Trust in God   Proverbs 3:5; Genesis 17:2, 4, 6; Genesis 22:12,
                      5, 2; Hebrews 11:6

Lightning Source UK Ltd.
Milton Keynes UK
UKHW010311080223
416649UK00009B/144/J